DEVELOPING MAJORS TAUGHT IN ENGLISH ONLY

国际经济与贸易全英文系列教材

国际商务：案例、阅读材料和练习集

INTERNATIONAL BUSINESS: CASES, READING MATERIALS AND EXERCISES

王佳芥 编著

西南财经大学出版社

图书在版编目(CIP)数据

国际商务:案例、阅读材料和练习集/王佳芥编著.—成都:西南财经大学出版社,2016.12
ISBN 978-7-5504-2766-2

Ⅰ.①国… Ⅱ.①王… Ⅲ.①国际商务—高等学校—教学参考资料
Ⅳ.①F740

中国版本图书馆 CIP 数据核字(2016)第 304413 号

国际商务:案例、阅读材料和练习集

GUOJI SHANGWU ANLI YUEDU CAILIAO HE LIANXIJI

王佳芥 编著

责任编辑	王 利
封面设计	张姗姗
责任印制	封俊川
出版发行	西南财经大学出版社(四川省成都市光华村街 55 号)
网 址	http://www.bookcj.com
电子邮件	bookcj@foxmail.com
邮政编码	610074
电 话	028-87353785 87352368
照 排	四川胜翔数码印务设计有限公司
印 刷	四川五洲彩印有限责任公司
成品尺寸	185mm×260mm
印 张	10.25
字 数	225 千字
版 次	2016 年 12 月第 1 版
印 次	2016 年 12 月第 1 次印刷
印 数	1—2000 册
书 号	ISBN 978-7-5504-2766-2
定 价	22.80 元

编者简介

王佳芥，女，西南财经大学国际商学院教师，比利时安特卫普大学管理学院国际管理硕士，德国政府奖学金——德国国际发展基金（Deutsche Stiftung für internationale Entwicklung，DSE）获得者。熟悉国际商务运营和资本运作，有丰富的国际商务和国际投融资的实战工作经验。成都市商务局外贸专家顾问。独立编写出版教材《国际商务：结合中国企业案例的分析》（58 万字），中国市场出版社，2010；独立编写全英文教辅《国际商务：案例、阅读材料和练习集》（22.5 万字），西南财经大学出版社，2016；第一主译《市场调研》（43 万字），中国市场出版社，2009；主译《游击营销》（40 万字），上海人民出版社，2010。四川省教育厅“高等教育本科课程体系改革——国际经济与贸易专业”省级课题负责人；西南财大全英文校级教改项目负责人；西南财大在线公开课程（慕课 MOOCs）在线主讲。

GENERAL PREFACE

China is currently endeavoring to move from a large trading power to a mighty one, and China's positive interaction between inward foreign direct investment (IFDI) and outward foreign direct investment (OFDI) gains momentum. The central government strategy of "One Belt, One Road" and "Mass Innovation and Entrepreneurship" provides China's foreign trade enterprises with a golden development opportunity, increases demand for international trade & business professionals who have social responsibility and are initiative, innovative, and international inter-disciplinary talents, and requires new and higher-quality standards for talent training in international trade speciality.

In order to implement the internationalization strategy of SWUFE, enhance the efficiency of internationalization of education, upgrade the level of education, and foster globally competitive talents, SWUFE launched a project of "Developing Majors Taught in English Only" in 2014. The project aims to reform the mode of latent training, cultivate initiative, innovative, and globally-competitive inter-disciplinary talents; develop a faculty who have advanced educational philosophy, state-of-the-art teaching methods, high-level teaching skills and teach courses with the English language only; establish an international educational curriculum system, gradually construct a series of high-quality courses taught in English only and geared to international standards; upgrade the training quality of overseas students at SWUFE; and comprehensively raise the level of SWUFE's internationalization of education. Also in 2014, the International Economics and Trade major of the School of International Business (SIB) was chosen among the first batch for the construction of the "majors taught in English only".

As part of English textbook construction project for "majors taught in English only", a series of English textbooks of International Economics and Trade major was launched in 2014. This series aims to solve three bottleneck problems of the construction of the International Economics and Trade major taught in English only. First, English textbooks are unavailable for some special degree courses with Chinese characteristics, e. g. *Introduction to China's Foreign Trade*. Second, many contents of imported English textbooks fail to meet with the requirements of training Chinese international economics and trade talents, for instance, *Trans-Culture Communication*. Third, imported foreign textbooks neither provide cases of Chinese enterprises, nor analyze internationalization experiences and strategies from a Chinese enterprise perspective. For instance, the popular textbook *International Business* is short of cases suitable for training

Chinese foreign economics and trade talents. As a response, in 2014, SIB launched 3 English textbooks *Introduction to China's Foreign Trade*, *Trans-Culture Communication*, *English for Finance and Economics Discipline*, and 1 complimentary English workbook *International Business: Cases, Reading Materials and Exercises*.

We hope this series of English textbooks assists the construction of English textbooks and workbooks for China's training international economics and trade talents. The series will also help foster the international trade & business talents with scientific attitude, humanistic quality, speciality skills and international orientation. With the deepening of "Developing Majors Taught in English Only", we will expand our series of international economics and trade textbooks in English.

PREFACE

International Business is quite a complex operation, involving an understanding of both the theoretical aspect and practical aspect. International Business comprises all commercial transactions (private and governmental, sales, investments, logistics, and transportation) that take place between two or more regions, countries and nations beyond their political boundaries. Usually, private companies undertake such transactions for profit; governments undertake them for profit and for political reasons. It refers to all those business activities which involve cross border transactions of goods, services, resources between two or more nations. Transaction of economic resources include capital, skills, people etc. for international production of physical goods and services such as finance, banking, insurance, construction etc.

Areas of study within this topic include differences in legal systems, political systems, economic policy, language, accounting standards, labor standards, living standards, environmental standards, local culture, corporate culture, foreign exchange market, tariffs, import and export regulations, trade agreements, FPI, FDI, TNCs management and many more topics. Each of these factors requires significant changes in how individual business units operate from one country to the next.

I would like to extend a personal welcome to you. Because the "International Business: Cases, Reading Materials and Exercises" provide a unique and excellent experience of and investigation into international business. In this case-study materials, we have invested hundreds of hours creating a series of dynamic and valuable resources for international business students, international business people and teachers at international business schools. We believe you'll find this case–study material is an excellent resource for a variety of your global business questions and needs, with particular focus on those topics unique to working in the international business arena.

International Business: Cases, Reading Materials and Exercises offers a well balanced program of cases, reading materials, on-line resources, discussion questions etc., providing a thorough understanding of international business and broader management subjects, which are then applied to the dynamics of an international environment. The program has been designed specifically to equip you with the knowledge, skills and in-filed tactics which you need to pursue a career in an international (or domestic) business setting, whether that means working with a large multi-national, a smaller company or even your own business. Teaching on the full-time program involves a combination of formal lectures, group discussions, tutorials, seminars and directed reading.

目 录

PART ONE
Amazing Introduction and Overview

CHAPTER 1
Amazing Introduction and Globalization

At the end of this chapter, you should be able to:

· Understand the amazing and challenges of international business;

· Understand the subject, the object, the scope of international business (5W);

· Understand the dual environmental pressures of international business;

· The term of globalization, its main driving forces and its pros and cons.

· The term of localization.

INTERNATIONAL BUSINESS focuses on International & Business. INTERNATIONAL concerned with Across Borders, which implies the subject and the object are quite different from domestic business. International business, Multinational, Transnational, Globalization, Multi domestic, Worldwide, and the Global Marketplace, these are the terms you deal with daily. In fact, the subject of international business are TNCs (Transnational Corporations) from worldwide (which implies international businesspersons are from different cultures, with not only different skin colors, but also different mentalities and behaviors). While the business geography covers 194 sovereignty states and regions. What's more, the main business modes of international business are far more complicated and diversified than domestic business, international business covers export/import, FDI/OFDI (foreign direct investment), FPI (foreign portfolio investment) and global foreign exchange market and capital market investment), global enterprises and business management. Meanwhile, Business is in fact a smokeless worldwide war, where the law of jungle dominates. All business types and activities are most complicated and demand professional skills and talents. We know international business success requires more business acumen than managing a domestic enterprise. You not only deal with traditional business functions and values, but also work from a global perspective that adds politics, culture, monetary variables, time, and distance to the international business management equation. That is why international businessperson are most-talented people from worldwide and just as Philip R. Cateora (international business lecturing tycoon) pointed out:

"The successful international businesspeople possesses the best qualities of the anthropologist, psychologist, diplomat, lawyer, Prophet and businessperson."

In this case-study materials of International Business, we have invested hundreds of hours creating a series of dynamic and valuable resources for international business students, international business people and teachers and professors at international business schools. We believe you'll find this case-study material is an excellent resource for a variety of your global business questions and needs, with particular focus on those topics unique to working in the International business arena.

Ⅰ. WHO

Discussion

1. Visit Fortune Magazine (www.fortune.com), consult the up-to-date ranking of Global 500. Please compare how the ranking list changed during recent years, especial the ranking of Chinese TNCs in 2015 and 2016; for example, State Grid (China) now ranks no. 2.

2. Please discuss with your partners the ranking criteria of Global 500 (for example, sales revenue, profit, or assets etc.); Why Global 500 ranking is decided by corporate sales revenue?

3. Please discuss with your partners the minimum entry barriers of Global 500; What's more, please use the data of minimum entry barriers to discuss the huge gaps between foreign TNCs and Chinese TNCs (for example, the scale, R&D, brand, channel, management etc.).

4. Take Exxon Mobile as an example, how the American petroleum giant companies evolved during the past century? (tip: from standard oil split-off in 1919 to the M&A in 1990s).

5. The following is up-to-date share price of Berkshire Hathaway Inc., please discuss why the share price can stay so high for decades.

BRK.A　未开盘 2016-09-19　16:00:00　EDT

218000.00

6. Discuss HON HAI PRECISION INDUSTRY (鸿海精密工业股份有限公司) from Taiwan and its subsidiaries in Mainland China.

Case: Senior VP- the Glass Ceiling of a Chinese in World Top TNCs

If we search the internet and pay a field visit to world top TNCs (Transnational Corporations), we will find that the number of top TNCs from China is increasing sharply. For example, according to www.fortunechina.com, there are 100 Chinese companies among the Top 500, Sinopec Group, with the annual sale revenue of USD 457.2 billion is even among the Top Three, just behind Walmart and Royal Dutch Shell. This is a historical ranking, and China in recent years is just behind of USA with 128 American companies are in Global Top 500.

But if we carry out further and deeper investigation on these 100 Chinese TNCs, we will find out the overwhelming majority is SOEs (State-Owned-Enterprises), among the 100 companies, only 7 if from private sectors.

What's more, if we examine the TNCs from abroad from example USA, EU and Japan, we will find that the role of Chinese is very limited. As the title of the case indicated, Senior VP (Senior Vice President) is the highest position a Chinese can achieve. For example, in 2003 Microsoft China appointed Mr. Gao Qunyao (高群耀) as the president of Microsoft China, in Microsoft Group, Mr. Gao is just a Senior VP. in 2009 Best Buy Co., Inc. (NYSE: BBY) (美国百思买集团), the world largest dealer chain for electronics products, merged and acquired Five-star Group (www.5star.cn), the No. 3 dealer chain for electronics products. Immediately after the M&A, Best Buy released news that Best Buy will appoint Mr. Wang Jianguo (汪建国), the chairman and CEO of Five-star Group, as the Senior VP of BBY. The same story happened to other western TNCs. For example, in 2004 Standard Chartered China (www.sc.com/cn) appointed Ms. Zeng jingxuan (曾璟璇) as President of Standard Chartered China, but in the SC Group worldwide, Ms. Zeng is just a Senior VP. In 2007, Mr. Qiu Zhizhong (邱致中) was appointed as the chairman of ABN AMRO (荷兰银行集团) China, if taking the title in a Chinese way, Mr. Qiu is a Senior VP in the group company.

Why there seems a glass ceiling for the Chinese in their career achievement in western TNCs? There are many reasons to explain. First, the strategic position of China is emerging, but not as important as many Chinese once believed. For example, for a long time, the sales revenue from Microsoft China was just like the figure of Microsoft Argentine. The General Electric China every year only got USD 5 billion sales revenue in China, only accounting for 3% of GE Group (its world sale revenue is about 150 billion USA annually). Second, historical background and development. Western TNCs grew up slowly and evolved over decades, even hundreds. So there are prestige families and prestige groups, the Chinese is just a new-comer for the whole group and can't challenge the existing organizational bureaucracy. There maybe other reasons behind and please discuss with your partners to find more out.

Discussion:

Take the ex-CEO of Walmart Stores (China), Mr. Chen Yaocang, as an example, please discuss the career path for the Chinese in Western TNCs. Why did Mr. Chen quit in 2011?

Reading Material: International Business Career Requirement

The global job market continues to be challenging, signs of a worldwide recovery raise expectations for new international job and career opportunities. If you are considering international business, here is a quick checklist to help you decide if you have the "right stuff".

1) Do you tend to be judgmental?

The single most important factor in working in another country on an international assignment is your ability to accept and work within the culture, customs, beliefs, and attitudes of that country. The majority of successful business executives achieve their success through a strong personality and making decisions based on their personal background and experience. However, when moving to another country, the executive is placed in a new environment where his or her background has little relationship to their new surroundings. The first reaction is frequently to take control of the situation and apply that strong personality. Nothing could be worse! The only way to be successful in an overseas assignment is through relationships that encourage the local employees to cooperate with the expatriate manager.

2) Do you enjoy people, or are you more task-oriented?

As a manager working in an international assignment, your primary job is certainly to accomplish the corporate goals and objectives. However, in many cultures throughout the world, the most important aspect of life is the support of the community, the people, the family. Unless there is a clear understanding of the motivations of employees, the manager may create animosity and jeopardize the productivity of the company's operation. It is strongly recommended that to learn everything possible about the culture you are potentially going into. A great place to start is with a detailed review of the GeertHofstede Cultural Dimensions for that country or region. You can access this information by selecting the country or region from the list on the left.

3) Are you flexible and welcome change?

Dealing with the unexpected is common in many countries, and can be especially challenging for U. S. managers who go overseas, since they are more accustomed to a relatively stabile business environment. The involvement of governments and politics in business is not unusual in many countries around the world, and especially in economically under-developed countries. The ability to be open to unexpected situations and challenges, some of which may be uncontrollable, is another important attribute for the international manager.

4) Do you like family and friends around you?

It is less likely in today's economic environment that companies will pay for full family relocation to foreign countries. More often, expatriate assignments are made with shorter term contracts of 12 - 18 months, rather than the older 2 - 3 year agreements. This allows the company to circumvent the more costly relocations. However, it is not unusual for one of these shorter term assignments to be extended before it ends. Therefore, many international assignments will require your ability to function effectively away from home, away from friends, and away from family for periods that may be extended up to 36 months. Another recent trend is extending the time interval between "home leave". Home leave is when an expatriate periodically returns home for one or two weeks. Again, these delays, or in some cases cancellations, are motivated by the company's desire to reduce costs and increase profitability.

5) Is it good news if your spouse can go with you?

This is a hard question to answer. Having a spouse on a foreign assignment certainly can be nice — If the spouse enjoys the assignment! In the majority of spousal relocations, it is not likely they can also be employed in the foreign country. So what do they do all day? Therefore, it is important that the spouse of an expatriate also answer each of the questions on this page, as he or she will be just as immersed in the new environment as an employee. In fact, overseas assignments are frequently much more difficult for the spouse because he or she is not working 10-12 hours a day, which easily fills the employee's time. For the spouse, sitting in a home or apartment in a country that may have a different language creates isolation, which can be a real problem.

6) How willing are you to take risks?

The world has become a more risky place for certain nationalities. In particular, citizens of theUnited States are considered legitimate targets by many international terrorist groups. While the chance of being injured by a terrorist act is very small, anti-American attitudes in many countries, including those that have been close allies, can make for a psychologically hostile and unhappy working and social environment.

Reference: Stephen Taylor. Considering an International Career. http: //international-business-careers. com/

Ⅱ. WHERE

The geography of international business covers worldwide, more than 194 sovereignty states and regions.

Reading Material: Diversified International Market: Middle East

Religion plays a very important role in all the countries of the middle east. The predominant religion for the Arab and middle eastern countries as well as Turkey, Afghanistan, Bangladesh, Pakistan, Djibouti, Gambia, Niger, Nigeria, Senegal, Somalia, Indonesia, Brunei and Malaysia is Muslim. Hindu is in the majolity in India, while a sizeable Muslim population exists.

Muslims follow the doctrines of the Koran, which forbids alcohol and the flesh of scavenger animals (i. e. pork). It also discourages use of caffeine and nicotine, although neither are forbidden; in fact, they tend to be consumed in great quantity in Arabic and Middle Eastern countries.

Avoid pork and pork products like ham, bacon, pate, hot dogs or sausage. Avoid food prepared with pork products like lard, which can include even pastries. It is a good idea to avoid any pork dishes at a banquet when Muslims are in attendance because the other dishes might become contaminated in preparation or serving. Fish is an acceptable alternative to meat and shellfish. Some Muslims prefer Zabihah meat which has been slaughtered according to special rules. Zabihah meat is similar too, but not the same as Kosher meat. Do not serve alcohol in the presence of guests, especially government or religious officials, from the more fundamentalist Muslim countries like Saudi Arabia or Kuwait, even if you know that the individual may drink in private. Many Muslims, however, do take exception to the rule forbidding alcohol. Pakistanis, for instance, are more liberal and frequently consume alcoholic beverages. But, it's best to err on the side of caution, especially in public. Serve fruit juices for toasts when alcoholic beverages cannot be consumed. Avoid food cooked in alcohol, even if all the alcohol has burned off in cooking. Muslims fast (斋戒) until sundown during the month of Ramadam.

Reference: http://www.international-business-etiquette.com/besite/mideast.htm

Discussion and exercises:

1. Please discuss with your partner the cultural difference between the Middle East and China.

2. Pleas pay much attention to the diversified middle east markets, for example, how do you differentiate a Persian state (such as Iran) from an Arabic state (such as UAE and Saudi Arabic). Can you understand the similarity and differences?

Ⅲ. WHAT: main business modes of international business

· export/import

· FDI/OFDI (foreign direct investment)

· FPI (foreign portfolio investment) and global foreign exchange market and capital market investment

· global enterprises and business management

Case: Export "Air" -China Carbon Market (2013)

China launched the first of its seven pilot emission-trading schemes (ETS) in Shenzhen on 18 June 2013. This marks China's creation of a carbon market with an emission cap to achieve its goal of reducing emission by 17% in the next two years and 40%~45% by 2020. The pilot ETS in Shenzhen is the first of seven planned pilot launches in 2013-2014. Five other regions - Beijing, Shanghai, Tianjin, Chongqing, and Guangdong - will begin their own pilot ETS later in 2013, and Hubei will commence its pilot in 2014. We believe we are the first on the way to conduct detailed research elaborating China's pilot and future carbon trading systems, roadmap, targets, agenda and risks.

A nationwide China ETS is planned for 2015 - 2016. Among the pilots, we believe Guangdong's ETS could emerge as the role model, given its diverse economic landscape, aggressive reduction target and a robust exchange designed for inter-provincial and international trading. Clean Development Mechanism (CDM) of the United Nations and Carbon Emission Reduction (CER) trading outside China have been the main drivers of China's renewable-energy development. After the plunge in carbon prices to below 1/ton (from 4/ton at the beginning of 2012), we think it is critical that ETS continues to provide incentives for China's renewable energy players with an initial carbon price of RMB 30/ton.

To be the second-largest carbon market globally. The pilot ETS aims to cover 600~700 million tons of CO_2 emissions, which could make China the second-largest carbon trading market in the world. NDRC - issued credits, called "China Certified Emission Reduction (CCER)", provide qualified offset credits. We think Chinese renewable operators (with wind operators likely to take 20% of the trading) should benefit from selling CCERs to companies with heavy carbon emissions.

Potential 8%~30% upside to wind operators' earning estimates. Our detailed scenario analysis indicates the possibility for an 8%~30% upside to our FY15E and FY16E EPS forecast for wind operators. We also estimate that these three companies could achieve 30~70 million tons carbon reduction in 2015-2016. We expect Datang Renewable to have the largest upside risk to earnings from potential carbon trading in China.

Uncertainties and challenges. Despite having built carbon trading infrastructure that includes national greenhouse gas (GHG) inventories, a rudimentary monitoring and verification standard, functioning trading exchanges and basic regulatory framework, there could still be insufficient legislations and third-party verification companies to support carbon trading in China. The key concern is that a simplistic approach could result in unfair allocation in which companies with historically high emission levels get higher quota while energy-efficient peers receive less than they deserve.

Appendix:

What is CDM?

The CDM is a mechanism for project-based emission reduction activities in developing countries. Certificates will be generated through the CDM from projects that lead to certifiable emissions reductions that would otherwise not occur. CDM is under the Kyoto Protocol (京都议定书), which was approved in 1997 and implemented in 2005.

The Kyoto protocol established binding greenhouse gas emissions reduction targets for 37 industrialised countries and the European community. To help achieve these targets, the protocol introduced three "flexible mechanisms" - international emissions trading (IET), joint implementation (JI), and the Clean Development Mechanism (CDM).

What is ETS?

The EU emissions trading system (EU ETS) is a cornerstone of the European Union's policy to combat climate change and its key tool for reducing industrial greenhouse gas emissions cost-effectively. The first - and still by far the biggest - international system for trading greenhouse gas emission allowances, the EU ETS covers more than 11 000 power stations and industrial plants in 31 countries, as well as airlines.

The EU ETS works on the "cap and trade" principle. A "cap", or limit, is set on the total amount of certain greenhouse gases that can be emitted by the factories, power plants and other installations in the system. The cap is reduced over time so that total emissions fall. In 2020, emissions from sectors covered by the EU ETS will be 21% lower than in 2005. By 2030, the Commission proposes, they would be 43% lower.

Reference: Macquarie Research: China carbon market (2013)

The EU Emissions Trading System (EU ETS) http://ec. europa. eu/clima/policies/ets/index_ en. htm

Discussion and Online Practices:

1. Please discuss with your partners a unique business mode: CARBON MARKET, its principles, practical operation as well as the uniqueness and difference from traditional business mode such as goods export?

2. Visit National Development and Reform Commission (国家发改委) http://www.sdpc.gov.cn/, then enter http://qhs. ndrc. gov. cn (“应对气候变化司”子站), click “CDM” and learn more info.

3. Visit the website of EU Emissions Trading System (EU ETS), www.europa.eu/clima/policies/ets, please study the mechanism from CDM to ETS. Please discuss how carbon market evolve during recent years?

4. Visit: www. carbonmarketdata. com/en/home, study the database and more info of global carbon market.

5. There are only two developed countries which didn't accept Kyoto Protocol: namely USA and Australia. What's your opinion of such strange phenomena?

Extended Reading:

1. Kyoto Protocol《京都议定书》

Note: Kyoto Protocol is supplementary provisions of United Nations Framework Convention on Climate Change, UNFCCC《联合国气候变化框架公约》;

2. Search the internet for: Macquarie Research: China carbon market (2013).

Ⅳ. HOW

How to carry out international business and how to acquire hands-on skills and experience in a business field. The following equation illustrate:

International Business = Science + Art +Workmanship

Extended Reading Book

Tycoon of international business: Sumantra Ghoshal (高沙尔);

2.

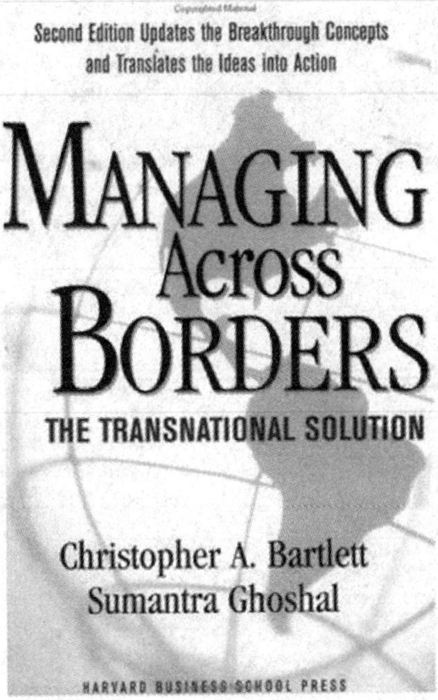

Managing Across Borders: *the Transnational Solution* (1998)

Ⅴ. WHY

The basic theoretical framework of international business.

Extended Reading Book

曾航：《一只 iPhone 的全球之旅》

Discussion:

The scope of globalization, the drives of globalization and its effects.

PART TWO
Country Difference

CHAPTER 2
National Differences in Political Economy

At the end of this chapter, you should be able to:

· Understand the localization difference in PEST model;

· How the political system differs worldwide;

· How the economic system and development differ worldwide;

· How the international business legal framework most complicated;

· How political and legal forces influences international business.

Case: Fight Between Dragon and Elephant (2012)
—Why India's telecom to snub Chinese companies in strategic co-op

The Department of Telecommunications (DoT) of India has called on New Delhi to "restrict Chinese presence only to telecom manufacturing while keeping strategic areas such as infrastructure and broadband networks for non-controversial countries like US, Japan, South Korea", Indian Express reported on Tuesday.

Being India's largest exporter of telecom goods, China was pushed to the lowest spot on a weighted assessment based on trade and strategic parameters. The move will seriously affect Chinese telecom firms' prospect of selling 3G wireless networks in India, observers say.

China got a very low strategic position in a 15-country international cooperation strategy prepared by the DoT. Chinese companies will only be given access to "telecom manufacturing".

The DoT report on strategically relevant countries was presented to Indian telecom minister Kapil Sibal on August 16. It recommends that key businesses such as infrastructure, broadband penetration, managing urbanization and resilient networks be assigned to the US, Japan, South Korea, Australia, Sweden and Finland while satellite and emergency communications be given to the US, Russia, Japan and France. Mobile applications would be sourced from the US, Japan, South Korea and Israel while cooperation in cloud computing would be restricted to the US and Japan only.

India will continue to allow imports of mobile phones, computer hardware like laptops and accessories such as USB dongles from China, but future Chinese sale of third-generation wireless broadband networks would be put in jeopardy, the Indian Express commented.

Joint working groups would be set up with the identified countries and relevant organizations to pursue the road map.

Since 2010, India has become "security conscious" and closely screens imports of network equipment. Equipment suppliers are required to make their software code and facilities available for inspection or, face penalty.

India and China held a meeting attended by commerce ministers of the two countries, during which China's telecom exports to India was a hotly contested topic. Market Watch said India is dissatisfied with the "widening" trade deficit as China has become its largest source of imports.

China-based Huawei Technologies and ZTE Corp. have big shares in India's mobile phone market. India has unveiled a series of counter measures, which, however, failed to produce significant impacts due to a huge and rigid demand for less costly China-made mobiles in the second most populous developing country.

In Sept. 2011, for another example, the mining ban in Karnataka, India has prompted Chinese buyers to identify new overseas markets for iron ore, trade sources said. The ban in Karnataka is likely to drag down the country's overall iron ore exports to abysmal levels.

What's more, the Visa Rule of India to the Chinese staffs and workers are extremely discriminatory. For example, the western staffs and workers can get a work via for more than years; but for the Chinese, India not only require so many complicated documents, but also often refuse to issue visa, or issue visa for just a few days, which is meaningless.

But India government and local society think the visa rule is reasonable and not a puzzle, because they think India has been most vulnerable to cross-border terrorism, and the 2008 attack on Mumbai Taj Mahal and Hilton hotels had shocked the whole nation, and it is still fresh in Indian memory. India's home minister had to resign and a new home minister, a graduate of Harvard Business School, was put in charge of the most sensitive ministry in India. Since then, travel to India has not been easy, especially for those who intend to travel on conference visas. A special approval from the Ministry of Home Affairs is required. Sometimes it really becomes a nightmare and one gets the visa hours before reporting at the airport. That is why in Feb. 2011, China urged that India should ease visa policy for Chinese. But, so far there has been no consideration.

Reference: Mei Jingya, Sina English. http://english.sina.com/world/2012/0828/501076.html

Mining ban sparks Chinese exit. http://www.indiaenvironmentportal.org.in/category/325/thesaurus/mining/

Binod Singh. India should ease visa policy for Chinese. http://www.chinadaily.com.cn/opinion/2011-02/16/content_12026214.htm

Discussion and exercises:

1. Why and How the geopolitical states, such as China & India conflict with each other frequently in international business arenas?

2. Why India frequently restrict Chinese TNCs, such as HUAWEI and ZTE etc.?

3. Please compare Sino-America EXIM with Hindu-America EXIM status.

Extension Case: Huawei Exit USA Forever (2013)? —Numerous Sufferings in America

On Oct. 18, 2012, the spokesman for Huawei criticized the report published by the Intelligence Committee of Americas House of Representatives. The report contains plenty of rhetoric about the supposed threats that Huawei and ZTE, the other Chinese company covered in it. But it is oddly devoid of hard evidence to support its draconian recommendations.

After its great success in Middle East and some European countries, Huawei aggressively targeted American market about 10 years ago. Maybe there were some progress in this efforts, but after decades, exploring, USA market seems is impenetrable.

Huawei caught the attention of American government and the public in 2007, when Huawei initiated to buyout 3com, but CFIUS denied the deal and 3com was bought by HP. In August 2012, Huawei planned to buyout 2wire or Motorola Wireless Department with value of more than USD billion 2. This time, Huawei suffered the same destiny, even Huawei's bid is much higher than competitors, but American government prefer British company to takeover 3com, and prefer Nokia from Finland to take over Motorola Wireless Department. Huawei took efforts in Amerca to smooth the American government and the public. For example, spent huge millions in Washington D. C. to carry out political lobby, and use commercial partners such as Motorola, but there seems no results.

What make worse is that American government urged its domestic large telecom corporations such as AT&T（美国电话电报公司）和 Verizon to but equipment from Huawei.

Dilemma and numerous sufferings, that's the reality Huawei faced in USA, that is why in August 2013, Huawei denounced the company will pay more attention to European market and exit America "STRATEGICALLY"!

Reference：华为开拓美国市场受阻 两宗交易均遭拒超10亿美元. http://www.s1979.com/news/tech/201008/035572803.shtml

华为宣布退出美国市场 将更重视欧洲市场. http://android.265g.com/yjzx/12184.html

李瀛寰. 征战企业网：华为和思科的那些事儿［EB/OL］. http://tech.sina.com.cn/zl/post/detail/t/2013-08-21/pid_8433237.htm

Discussion:

1. Please discuss why Huawei always suffered deny of various buyout and deny in American market. What are the political reasons behind?

2. In 2012, Sanyi Heavy Industrial Co. Ltd.（三一重工）successfully buyout the world top concrete brand company -Putzmeister, Germany. Please compare the success case of Sanyi in Germany with the failure case of Huawei in USA. Please discuss why EU becomes the No. 1 Technology outsourcing place for China.

3. There is a saying that Cisco（思科）, the American giant as well as the main rivalry of Huawei, played an important role of denying and attacking Huawei. [Cisco is the inventor of Router（路由器）and the core switching node. Please compare the two companies.] How do you look at this saying?

Case：Ecuador Confiscated 99% Oil Profit of Foreign Companies —Windfall Profits Tax Law（石油暴利税法）(2005/2008)

Ecuador has had one of the most volatile oil policies in the region, partly a reflection of the high political volatility in the country. Petroecuador accounts for over half of oil production, however, as a result of financial setbacks combined with a drop in oil price, private companies increased oil investments in Ecuador. In the early 1990s annual foreign investment in oil was below US $ 200 million, by the early 2000s it had surpassed US $ 1 billion (Campodónico, 2004). Changes in political power led to an increase in government control over oil extraction. In particular, the election of President Rafael Correa, on a resource-nationalism platform, prompted increases in government control and the approval of a windfall profits tax, which is 99% of oil profit of foreign companies, including CNPC (www.cnpc.com.cn) and Sinopec (www.sinopec.com).

The nationalisation of oil supplies refers to the process of confiscation of oil production operations and private property, generally in the purpose of obtaining more revenue from oil for oil producing countries' governments. This generally unlawful process, which should not be confused with restrictions on crude oil exports, represents a significant turning point in the development of oil policy. Nationalization eliminates private business operations—in which private international companies control oil resources within oil-producing countries—and allows oil-producing countries to gain control of private property, often in violation of existing agreed-upon legal contracts. Once these countries become the sole owners of these confiscated resources in violation of contract law, they have to decide how to maximize the net present value of their known stock of oil in the ground. Several key implications can be observed as a result of oil nationalization. On the home front, national oil companies are often torn between national expectations that they should carry the flag and their own ambitions for commercial success, which might mean a degree of emancipation from the confines of a national agenda

According to consulting firm PFC Energy, only 7% of the world's estimated oil and gas reserves are in countries that allow private international companies free rein. Fully 65% are in the hands of state-owned companies such as Saudi Aramco, with the rest in countries such as Russia and Venezuela, where access by Western companies is difficult. The PFC study implies political groups unfavorable to capitalism in some countries tend to limit oil production increases in Mexico, Venezuela, Iran, Iraq, Kuwait and Russia. Saudi Arabia is also limiting capacity expansion, but because of a self-imposed cap, unlike the other countries.

In March 2011, ConocoPhillips（美国康菲石油公司）reported that In 2008, Burlington

Resources, Inc., a wholly owned subsidiary of ConocoPhillips, initiated arbitration before ICSID (the World Bank's International Centre for Settlement of Investment Disputes, or ICSID) against the Republic of Ecuador and PetroEcuador, as a result of the newly enacted Windfall Profits Tax Law and government-mandated renegotiation of our production sharing contracts. Despite a restraining order issued by ICSID, Ecuador confiscated the crude oil production of Burlington and its co-venturer and sold the illegally seized crude oil. In 2009, Ecuador took over operations in Blocks 7 and 21, fully expropriating our assets. In June 2010, the ICSID tribunal concluded it has jurisdiction to hear the expropriation claim. An arbitration hearing on case merits occurred in March 2011. The arbitration process is ongoing.

In 2007, ConocoPhillips announced they had been unable to reach agreement with respect to our migration to an empresa mixta structure mandated by the Venezuelan government's Nationalization Decree. As a result, Venezuela's national oil company, PDVSA, or its affiliates directly assumed control over ConocoPhillips' interests in the Petrozuata and Hamaca heavy oil ventures and the offshore Corocoro development project. In response to this expropriation, ConocoPhillips filed a request for international arbitration on November 2, 2007, with the ICSID. An arbitration hearing was held during 2010 before ICSID, and the arbitration process is ongoing.

If you visit the website of ICSID (the World Bank's International Centre for Settlement of Investment Disputes) www. icsid.worldbank.org, please click the case, then check the concluded cases and pending cases, there are numerous exploitation and exploration, confiscation and nationalization cases during the past century.

Reference: http://en.wikipedia.org/wiki/Nationalization_of_oil_supplies

http://www.sec.gov/Archives/edgar/data/1163165/000095012311043802/h80298e10vq.htm

https://icsid.worldbank.org/ICSID/FrontServlet? requestType=GenCaseDtlsRH&actionVal=ListConcluded

Discussion:

1. What are your comments on the 99% windfall tax?

2. Now Chinese petroleum giants face dilemma: stick to Ecuador and accept the exploitation and injustice fate, or spin off local business and suffer huge loss. What is you opinion?

3. Take another Latin-American state as an example, Venezuela since 2006 adopted USD 50 billion supporting loans from China and now is experiencing default crisis. What do you think of the political risks and economic risks in LA?

Extension Case: Grey Customs Clearance Leads Chinese Businesspeople to Bankruptcy (2009)

Chinese businesspeople who travel thousands of miles to the Russian capital have mixed feelings towards the local market. "We are both thrilled and scared." Shoe-producer Yu Jinhua put it with telling brevity. Yu, the general manager of the Wenzhou Jierda Shoes Co

Ltd, in East China's Zhejiang Province, says that 60 per cent of the leather shoes made by his company go to Russia. However, over the past five years, Yu has suffered great economic losses in Russia because of the so-called "grey customs clearance".

The "grey customs clearance" started in the early 1990s amidst the social confusion arising from the downfall of the Soviet Union. Faced with a shortage of commodities, the Customs Committee of Russia, in an effort to encourage import trade and simplify customs procedures, allowed its so-called "customs clearance companies" to provide one-stop services that covered both transportation and customs clearance procedures. These companies, with close relations with Russian customs and backed up by influential figures in Russia, enjoy many privileges. They normally do not supply customs clearance manifests, which means that importers who use their services are often suspected of smuggling.

It is not only Chinese businesspeople who go to the "customs clearance companies" in order to cut costs and, more importantly, to improve efficiency; their counterparts from Turkey, the Republic of Korea, Spain and other countries also follow the same practice.

Statistics from Russian Customs indicate that commodities entering Russia through the "grey customs clearance" route make up about 30 per cent of the private trade volume between China and Russia. Commodities involved include garments, shoes and hats, and suitcases and bags. But imported commodities without proper customs documents will be confiscated. Chinese businesspeople suffered in this unpredictable market. Russia market is not stable and we are exposed to high risks. Russian police raided Chinese retail outlets more than 100 times checking for legal customs clearance documents. Chinese businesses suffer from such raids, their goods are confiscated and they paid huge fines, many Chinese businesspeople went bankruptcy.

Reference: Time to stop "grey customs clearance" (China Daily): 2004-05-28 1http://www.chinadaily.com.cn/english/doc/2004-05/28/content_334708.htm

Discussion:

1. Please discuss how the global business environment (especially legal and political framework) affect business?

2. Please discuss overseas political risks suffered by international business (for example, confiscation, expropriation and nationalization). Are there any approaches to predict the political risks in a specific country? Can you provide some measure which can lower the political risks?

3. How TNCs evaluate the political risks in international business as well as approaches to lower the risks. Can you give some examples?

Extended Reading and Online Practices:

1. Visit the website of Overseas Investment Company of US (美国海外投资保险公司) www.opic.org, study how the American government help to cover the overseas political risks of American enterprises (political risks policy, different insurances, its coverage, rates etc.).

Please discuss with partners how China can learn from American practices.

2. Visit the website of ICSID (the World Bank's International Centre for Settlement of Investment Disputes) www. icsid.worldbank.org, learn its rule of dispute settlement, the recent typical cases (including concluded cases and pending cases) etc.

3. Please visit Ministry of Commerce of the People's Republic of China (www.mofcom.gov.cn), and study the international business policies and laws of Iran, Cuba and India etc, these countries historically experienced large-scale confiscation on foreign companies. How their policies evolved and up-to-date attitude towards foreign trade and investment nowadays.

Case: TCM Firm Tries to Survive EU Ban (2011)

As Traditional Chinese Medicine (TCM) is expanding its presence in the global market, European Union (EU) herbal directive could be a stumbling block on the road. As the world's biggest herbal medicine market, the European Union has recorded an annual herbal medicine turnover of about 10 billion euros, more than 40 percent of the world's total. The EU released the "Registration Process Order of Traditional Herbal Medicine" in March 2004, ordering that Chinese pharmaceutical enterprises will have to retreat from the EU market if their patented medicinal products have not been registered in EU countries by April 2011. So far, no Chinese firm has succeeded in obtaining a product license from an EU country.

The EU rules dictate that traditional herbal medicines cannot be licensed unless they have been in use for 30 years and have experienced a 15 year presence in the EU market. However, many of the traditional Chinese medicines sold in the EU market were registered as "dietary supplements" rather than drugs at customs before 2004. Therefore, most of the pharmaceutical enterprises cannot provide valid evidence to prove the presence of their medicinal products in the EU market. Meanwhile, to be licensed by EU countries, the enterprises will have to be able to introduce the exact chemical compositions and functions of medicinal products to the EU authorities. But Traditional Chinese Medicine is an empirical science, which means the clinical efficacy and the chemical composition of the drugs can hardly be explained in scientific terms. Additionally, the registration application fees are too high for Chinese companies.

With a history of more than 2 000 years, TCM did not enter into the EU market until mid-1990s, and it has been imported into the EU and sold to European customers as food supplements instead of drugs. Historically herbal medicinal products, most of which have been sold as food supplements for decades in the EU market, will no longer be allowed unless they have obtained a medicine license, according to the EU Traditional Herbal Medicinal Products Directive adopted in 2004. The directive introduced a so-called simplified registration procedure with a seven-year transition period for traditional herbal medicinal products to be licensed, including Chinese and Indian traditional medicines. No single Chinese herbal medicinal product has been granted the license.

Reference: Miao Xiaojuan, Shang Jun. TCM global presence challenged by EU herbal directive. 2011 - 04 - 30 http://news.xinhuanet.com/english2010/health/2011 - 04/30/c_13852439.htm

TCM firm tries to survive EUban. China Daily. 2011-04-17. http://www.chinadaily.com.cn/china/2011-04/17/content_12340437.htm

Discussion:

1. How foreign legal framework affects, even bans international business?

2. Why the TCM firms failed to comply with the EU new regulation?

CHAPTER 3 Difference in Culture

At the end of this chapter, you should be able to:

- Know the whole concept of culture;
- Identify the five forceswhich sharp the cultural difference;
- Geert Hofstede Cultural Dimensions;
- Cultural shock andIntercultural management.

Case: Gay Wife of Iceland's Female Prime Minister Visits Beijing (2013) &Saudi Arabia Bans "Gays, Tom-boys" from Schools (2012)

Edward Tylor (1870) said that "Culture is the complex whole which includes knowledge, belief, art, morals, custom, and other capabilities acquired by man as a member of society".

The cores of diversified cultures are different, the values, norms, folkways and mores are quite different. Violation of the values and norm etc. can bring serious retribution or punishment. For example, the behavior such as theft, adultery, incest and cannibalism etc. will experience completely different result. For example, if the adultery is a caught in Middle East, the local culture and society will carry out "Honor Murder"(荣誉谋杀) of the two persons. In other country, such adultery is just a matter of moral issue.

Understanding the culture in a country or region in which you are doing business is a critical skill for the international business person. Without this knowledge, a successful outcome to the business venture can be in jeopardy.

The following case illustrate how different cultures treat the same behaviors differently, for example, the gay and lesbian society.

Jonina Leosdottir, the gay wife of Iceland's prime minister, took centre stage this week at a reception in her honour during a visit to the Beijing Foreign Studies University (BFSU), but her sexuality was largely off the table in discussions with students.

Women in the Nordic countries are equal to men. Nordic women have full-time jobs, they look after the children and the home, and even take part in politics. Nordic countries are unique across worldwide for numerous powerful female politicians such as premier, present, ministers. What's more, the gay and lesbian community as well as homosexual marriage are legal. For example, on June 27, 2010, Iceland verify homo-marriage and Iceland's premier and her spouse, Jonina Leosdottir, became the first legal homo-spouse in Iceland.

By sharp contrast, on April 16, 2012, Saudi Arabia has decided to bar "gays and tomboys" from its government schools and universities within a crackdown against the spread of this phenomenon in the conservative Moslem Gulf Kingdom. The Commission for the Promotion of Virtue and Prevention of Vice, the most feared law enforcement authority in the oil-rich country, has been asked to enforce the new orders. Instructions have been issued to all public schools and universities to ban the entry of gays and tom boys and to intensify their efforts to fight this phenomenon, which has been promoted by some websites. High-level orders have been issued to the Commission to immediately enforce the new rules and to step up efforts to combat this phenomenon and other "unacceptable behavior" in public places.

Case: "Happy Life" of Norway Mass Killer (2011)

It's the world's worst killing, in 90 minutes of madness, 32-year-old Anders Behring Breivik killed 69 young people. Faced with the worst crimes on its territory since World War Ⅱ, many in Norway have been dismayed by the prospect that the perpetrator could serve just 21 years behind bars, the maximum sentence allowed for the terrorism charges he currently faces. According to Foreign Policy's Robert Zeliger, most murderers in Norway serve 14 years or less. What's more, the lawyer for Anders Behring Breivik, who has admitted to carrying out Friday's mass killings in Norway, says his client believes his killings were necessary to spark an anti-Muslim revolution in Europe.

What shocked the whole world is not only just 21 years imprisonment, which means one life only cost 3 months imprisonment; but also the cold-blooded killer now lands in the world's most luxurious prison. The prison opened in 2010 outside of Oslo and houses around 250 male inmates. Each cell of the prison are equipped with an en-suite bathroom, a flat-screen TV and various comforts. They measure 12 [square meters—about 129 square feet and are divided up into units (10 to 12) which share a living room and kitchen, much like a college dorm. *Time Magazine* described the cells as resembling an Ikea showroom, complete with "stainless-steel countertops, wraparound sofas and birch-colored coffee tables." The art budget for the facility came in at more than a million dollars, Masi says, while the cells are brightly painted and lack bars on the windows. Inmates take specialty cooking classes or choose from many other courses at an in-prison high school. They can jog around the 75-acre wooded facility or even climb on the prison's rock walls.

Prison guards are required to help each inmate make his sentence "as meaningful, enlightening and rehabilitating as possible". About half of the prison guards are women, since research has suggested that a corps of female guards can help reduce aggression among the prison population. The unarmed guards eat meals and play games with prisoners. Anders Behring Breivik even applied the Oslo University and got admission, because the university authority have no power and excuse to deny his applicantion.

Reference: Norway mass killer likely insane: lawyer. http://www.abc.net.au/news/

2011-07-26/lawyer-says-norway-killer-likely-insane/2811550

Could accusedNorway killer land in luxurious prison? http://news.yahoo.com/blogs/lookout/accused-norway-killer-may-land-luxurious-prison-173329040.html

Discussion:

1. Please use the above various cases to discuss with your partners the diversity of different cultures worldwide.

2. How these cultural diversity influence the carry out of international business?

3. SCR (Self-reference Criteria, 自我参照标准) and ethnocentrism (民族优越感) are used to describe the cultural limits of international business, such as the businesspeople failed to understand and adapt to differences prevalent in foreign markets. Can you discuss with your partners the possible solutions which can overcome SCR?

Extended Reading Book:

Asian Godfathers. Joe Studwell. Fudan University Press. ISBN: 978730908234

Discussion and Exercises:

1. How the East Asian's business context is based on reciprocal relationship networks ?

2. Can you apply the Confucius doctrine to the real business practices?

3. China National Petroleum Corporation (CNPC, 中石油) choose Neil Bush, the little brother of Gorge W. Bush, as the global M&A ambassador. Neil Bush do represent CNPC and successfully buyout huge oil fields. What are your comments on this scenario?

4. Search theYale's elite secret society, Skull and Bones. How elite culture affect international business?

Extended Reading: Geert Hofstede Cultural Dimensions-Fact or Farce ?

It happens somewhere in the world everyday. Negotiations have been accelerating and both sides seem to be nearing a fruitful culmination. The end is in sight when suddenly it begins to unravel. Perhaps impatience to "close" was the trigger, or frustration that one side seemed to be "back pedaling". Whatever the reason is, the deal has fallen apart.

Perhaps one of the most difficult aspects of international business is dealing with, and understanding, differences in culture. Learning the international business etiquette and manners in details will benefit a lot.

Geert Hofstede's world famous studies and analysis of cultural differences. The Hofstede analysis graphs are presented for each of the countries, giving the global business person better insights to diversity. Geert Hofstede conducted one of the most comprehensive studies of how values in the workplace are influenced by culture. He analyzed a large database of employee value scores collected within IBM between 1967 and 1973. The data covered more than 70 countries, from which Hofstede first used the 40 countries with the largest groups of respondents and afterwards extended the analysis to 50 countries and 3 regions. Subsequent studies validating the earlier results include such respondent groups as commercial airline pilots and students in 23 countries, civil service managers in 14 counties, "up-market" consumers in 15 countries and "elites" in 19 countries.

In recent years the work of Dr. Geert Hofstede and his cultural dimensions has been carefully reviewed by academic scholars and educators around the world. As a result of this more careful analysis and scrutiny there are now questions, and in some cases open criticism of the assumptions Geert Hofstede utilized in arriving at his conclusions and theories. In order to assist international business students, professors, and teachers arrive at their own independent decisions on whether Geert Hofstede's work is valid, the website, http://geert-hofstede.com/, is great helpful to examine the validity of the cultural dimension. Useful tools from the website include: culture compass, Mobile Apps etc.

Discussion:

1. The dimension of Hofstede is under continuous examination, verification and challenges. Can you search proper country cases which can support and/or undermine the conclusion of this model? For example, question the conclusion: Is Japan a masculine society?

International Success Tips: Business Meeting Gifts

Preparing for a business meeting requires a working knowledge of the information to be discussed or presented, careful attention to all details on the printed material to be distributed, and perhaps a gift.

This gift is a social gesture that may be expected in some countries, and could be considered a bribe in others. Knowing the gift guidelines for the country you'll be visiting will help make your meeting a success. Some multi-national companies and some governments have very strict policies regarding their employees accepting gifts. To avoid creating a problem, it's imperative you learn the policies for the companies you do business with.

Countries like Malaysia and Paraguay, concerned with corruption, frown upon any gift that could be construed as a bribe. In Malaysia you wouldn't give a gift until you had established a relationship with the person. In Singapore, government employees are not allowed to accept gifts, and the United States limits the acceptable dollar value to $ 25. However, in some countries like Japan, Indonesia and the Philippines, exchanging gifts is strongly rooted in tradition. Part of the tradition is the gracious style used to present and receive them. It's important to plan time and focus on the process. It's very important in Asia and the Middle East to only use your right hand, or both hands, to offer or accept a gift. In Japan, use both hands. In Singapore a recipient may "graciously refuse three times" before accepting your gift. But in Chile, gifts are accepted and opened immediately. And in Indonesia, small gifts are given on a frequent basis. Always be cognizant of religious laws when selecting gifts. For instance, pork is prohibited in the Jewish and Muslim religions, so you wouldn't select a gift made from pigskin. As in India, don't offer a gift made from cowhide. Another prohibition for the Muslim faith is alcohol.

A standard to keep in mind for any gift you select is quality. Choose quality items that are not ostentatious. If you have gifts with your company logo, it's better if the logo is discreet. And don't give company logo gifts in Greece, Spain and Portugal. Hosting a meal at a nice restaurant is always a good business practice. A fine dinner is a wonderful way to give a "gift to your hosts", to show your guests you appreciate the business relationship you have with them, and an opportunity to build rapport. People in Brazil, England, Panama, and Peru enjoy being invited guests for a meal, and the Greeks look forward to an evening filled with dining. In China, plan a banquet, especially if you are being honored with one. Should you receive a gift, and don't have one to offer in return, you will not create a crisis. However, this is a good reason for planning to host a meal.

For a typical example from the Muslim culture, the Koran forbids alcohol. Gifts of liquor or any product that contains alcohol, such as perfume, would never be selected to give. Also, forbidden are products or foods from scavengers, which includes pork, birds, and shellfish. So a leather item made from pigskin or ostrich could not be given, nor any food from these groups. Other categories are also not appropriate for gifts. These include personal clothing items, which are far too personal to give as gifts. Dogs are considered unclean, so any dog item, even something with a picture of a dog would not be given. And knives because they have a sharp edge severing relationships - are not appropriate. Artwork that consisted of sculptures, drawings or photos showing the human body, especially a nude or partially nude female body, is not acceptable as a gift. And although nicotine is discouraged, It is frequently used in the Arabic and Middle Eastern countries.

A good gift for a devout Muslim is a compass. Each day he must face Mecca for prayers. With a compass, no matter where in the world he happens to be, he can easily find the correct direction. If you are in a country that were not predominantly Muslim, and you should be entertaining Muslim business associates, select a restaurant that serves halal food. And don't have alcohol served, especially if any government or religious officials are attending, even if you know your guests may drink in private. It is far better to stay more conservative when entertaining. Gifts are presented using the right hand, or both hands. The left hand is never used alone to hand someone a gift, as it is considered unclean. In the Muslim culture, the Koran forbids alcohol.

Reference: Kimberley Roberts. Business Meeting Gifts. http://international-business-center.com/international_business_gifts_greetings.html

Discussion:

In many developed countries such as USA, the value can't exceed 25 USD, otherwise bribery. Please discuss with your partners about the proper gifts in international business.

CHAPTER 4
Ethics in International Business

At the end of this chapter, you should be able to:

- Identify the main ethic issues in international business;
- Learn the corruption and bribery rules worldwide and its legal regulatory framework;
- Discuss the main ethical dilemma TNCs facesworldwide;
- Understand the different philosophical approaches to ethics.

Case: Underlying Rules of TNCs:
—Bribery Scandals: GSK (2013) VS Siemens (2008)

August 2013, UK-based drug maker Glaxo Smith Kline (GSK) was accused of giving bribes to doctors in China. China's investigation into the operations of UK pharmaceutical giant Glaxo Smith Kline and other multinational drug companies shows that the government is serious about tackling corruption and commercial misbehavior. But it also exposed a rotten core in the nation's medical system that needs to be addressed. Sinohealth Intelligence pointed out in a research report that 74 percent of pharmaceutical sales emanated from hospitals.

GSK is not a unique case. On December 15, 2008, SIEMENS, the German engineering giant, agreed to pay a record total of $ 1.6 billion to American and European authorities to settle charges that it routinely used bribes and slush funds to secure huge public works contracts around the world. The company also pleaded guilty in federal court in Washington to charges that it violated a 1977 law banning the use of corrupt practices in foreign business dealings. The fines that the company agreed to pay on the American side of the case — $ 450 million to the Justice Department and $ 350 million to the Securities and Exchange Commission — dwarf the previous high for a foreign corruption case brought by Washington. That mark of $ 33 million was set last year in the case of Baker Hughes, an oil conglomerate that paid a total of $ 44 million over foreign bribery charges. Officials said that Siemens, beginning in the mid-1990s, used bribes and kickbacks to foreign officials to secure government contracts for projects like a national identity card project in Argentina, mass transit work in Venezuela, a nationwide cellphone network in Bangladesh and a United Nations oil-for-food program in Iraq under Saddam Hussein. "Their actions were not an anomaly," said Joseph Persichini Jr., the head of the Washington office of the Federal Bureau of Investigation. "They were standard operating procedures for corporate executives who viewed bribery as a business strategy."

SIEMENS' bribery scandal has spread to China, after hitting its operations in Germany, Switzerland, Italy, Greece, the United States and Russia in 2008. Siemens has been rocked by investigations by German and U. S. authorities into suspected bribery involving hundreds of millions of euros. Last month, it said it was extending its internal investigation into the bribery issue.

China is a major growth driver for Siemens, which makes a wide range of products in the country, from industrial automation systems to washing machines and hearing aids. The German conglomerate said that it had invested more than 15 billion RMB ($ 2 billion) in China and planned to invest a further 10 billion RMB, doubling its annual sales in 2010 from 50. 4 billion RMB in 2006. Shenzhen Metro relies on Siemens' technologies although there is no suggestion the city's transport company is involved in the bribery allegations. Siemens received new orders worth RMB 5. 6 billion from China in 2005, a 34 percent jump from a year before. Its sales volume jumped 15 percent to RMB 44. 3 billion in the year.

Reference: GSK in bribery scandal. http://english.peopledaily.com.cn/90778/8350806. html

Siemens bribery scandal hitsChina. http://paper.sznews.com/szdaily/20070830/ca2760145. htm

Extended Reading: Foreign Corrupt Practices Act (1977)

The Foreign Corrupt Practices Act of 1977 (FCPA) is a United States federal law known primarily for two of its main provisions, one that addresses accounting transparency requirements under the Securities Exchange Act of 1934 and another concerning bribery of foreign officials.

The FCPA applies to any person who has a certain degree of connection to the United States and engages in foreign corrupt practices. The Act also applies to any act by U. S. businesses, foreign corporations trading securities in the United States, American nationals, citizens, and residents acting in furtherance of a foreign corrupt practice whether or not they are physically present in the United States. In the case of foreign natural and legal persons, the Act covers their actions if they are in the United States at the time of the corrupt conduct. Further, the Act governs not only payments to foreign officials, candidates, and parties, but any other recipient if part of the bribe is ultimately attributable to a foreign official, candidate, or party. These payments are not restricted to just monetary forms and may include anything of value.

United Nations Convention Against Corruption (2005)

The United Nations Convention against Corruption (UNCAC) is a multilateral convention negotiated by members of the United Nations. It is the first global legally binding international anti-corruption instrument. In its 71 Articles divided into 8 Chapters, UNCAC requires that States Parties implement several anti-corruption measures which may affect their laws, institutions and practices. These measures aim at preventing corruption, criminalizing certain conducts, strengthening international law enforcement and judicial cooperation, providing effective legal mechanisms for asset recovery, technical assistance and information exchange, and mechanisms for implementation of the Convention, including the Conference of the States Parties to the United Nations Convention against Corruption (COSP).

Reference: http://en.wikipedia.org/wiki/United_Nations_Convention_against_Corruption

Discussion:

1. Ethics issues in international trade and CSR (corporate social responsibility) of TNCs.

2. Since 1970s, bribery by Americancompanies will incur harsh criminal and monetary punishment. In 1990s, OECD members states forbid their TNCs to offer bribery to ensure the success of international business worldwide. But why TNCs from America carry our bribery in developing countries such as China?

3. Siemens used a wide network of front companies, mostly in Liechtenstein and the United Arab Emirates. Please search internet to carry out further investigation on the main network/ channels /platforms of offering and taking bribery as well as innovation of such behaviors.

4. In FCPA, the act allows a special kind of facilitating or expediting payments (grease payment) to secure the performance of a routine governmental action. Please discuss the difference between a bribery and a grease payment?

Online Practices:

1. Visit www.transparency.org, consult the ranking of CPI (corruption perception index 2014) as well as read more infield investigation and report of global corruption.

2. Visit www.ethisphere.com, please search "worlds-most-ethical/wme-honorees" (全球最具道德企业排行榜).

3. Visit www.csr-china.net.

Extended Reading: What Is a Country's "Corruption Perception Index" (CPI)?

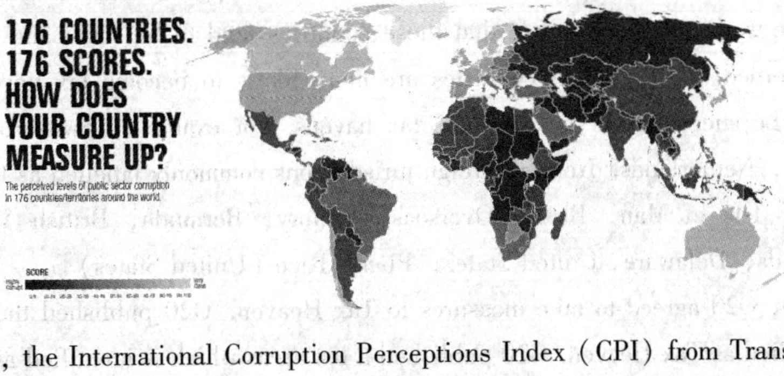

In 2014, the International Corruption Perceptions Index (CPI) from Transparency International has been released. Transparency International is a NGO based in Berlin, Germany. The report charts the perceived level of corruption in each of 176 countries. By utilizing a process of surveying perceptions by business people, academics and risk analysts, of the degree of corruption within a country, the numeric indexes will range between 10 (highly clean) and 0 (highly corrupt).

So what are the results for this year? At the top of the list was Denmark, Finland, and Sweden with a CPI Index score of 90, followed by Sweden with 88 and Singapore at 87. At the other end of the scale, and considered the most corrupt nations on earth is Somalia, North Koreas, and Afghanistan at 8 with Sudan at 13 and Myanmar at 15, followed by Turkmenistan and Uzbekistan at 17. The report makes for good reading, and an excellent topic for discussion among international business managers, always concerned about risk, and the best way to hedge against potential losses. Also of note is that the first Corruption Perception Index in 1995 had the United States at 78 (78 under new 0~100 scale). Now, 19 years later in 2014, the perceived corruption in the US has increased by 6.4% to a current CPI of 73. Before your next visit and negotiation session in any country, perhaps it may be advantageous to look up the Corruption Perception Index? To review the complete listing of the Corruption Perceptions Index, including the methodology used, go to one of these locations: You can view the CPI Table at this LINK www.transparency.org; you can download the full eight CPI report in Acrobat PDF at this LINK.

Case: Deadline of Global Tax Heavens (2010)

A tax heaven is a state, country or territory where certain taxes are levied at a low rate or not at all. Individuals or corporate entities can find it attractive to establish shell subsidiaries or move themselves to areas with reduced or nil taxation levels relative to typical international taxation. This creates a situation of tax competition among governments. Different jurisdictions tend to be havens for different types of taxes, and for different categories of people or companies. States that are sovereign or self-governing under international law have theoretically unlimited powers to enact tax laws affecting their territories, unless limited by previous international treaties.

The U. S. National Bureau of Economic Research has suggested that roughly 15% of the countries in the world are tax havens, that these countries tend to be small and affluent, and that better governed and regulated countries are more likely to become tax havens, and are more likely to be successful if they become tax havens. For example, Switzerland, Luxembourg, Ireland, Netherlands. Non-sovereign jurisdictions commonly labelled as tax havens include: Jersey, Isle of Man, British Overseas Territory, Bermuda, British Virgin Islands [Cayman Islands, Delaware, United States, Puerto Rico (United States)].

May 2010, G20 agreed to take measures to Tax Heaven. G20 published the list of areas which is identified as Tax Heaven. G20 published a list areas which is identified as tax heaven, classified as black list, grey areas, white list. G20 take measures to tax heaven including: cancel banking secrecy step by step; cancel the investments in tax heaven which is given by IMF and World Bank; require to release bank and tax info to G20, and cooperate with exchange of information. The deadline is May 2010, thoes who refused to obey G20rules will suffer harsh punishment from G20 and OECD.

For example, Switzerland is not safe since 2009. Due to the pressure and urge from USA, Swiss government had to amend the Constitution and release band account information to FBI and IRS (Internal Revenue Service, 美国国税局). Since 2010, Hong Kong and Macau became the off-list of OECD because of their actively cooperation with OECD.

Reference: http://en.wikipedia.org/wiki/Tax_haven

Extension Case: Foreign Account Tax Compliance Act (FATCA) 2014 (肥猫法)

The Foreign Account Tax Compliance Act (FATCA) is a piece of USA legislation and part of the United States (US) Hiring Incentives to Restore Employment (HIRE) Act. It was signed into US law on 18 March 2010.

FATCA imposes a reporting system on US taxpayers holding financial assets outside the US, requiring them to report those assets to the US Internal Revenue Service (IRS). Meanwhile, foreign financial institutions (FFIs) are also required to report certain information directly to the IRS about financial accounts held by USA taxpayers, or by foreign entities in which USA taxpayers hold a substantial ownership interest.

The key objective of US FATCA is to ensure that theUS tax authorities are collecting the appropriate amount of tax from all USA persons by identifying all assets held by US persons, in FFIs outside of the United States. What is UK FATCA?

In 2013, the UK tax authorities announced that a similar FATCA regime would be enacted in relation to UK persons and it is likely that other countries will follow.

In October 2013 the UK entered into Intergovernmental Agreements ("IGAs") with its Crown Dependencies. These IGAs are based on the USA-UK IGA to reduce the compliance burden and provide consistency. As the IGAs are all very similar, the draft guidance for implementation has been released jointly by the three Crown Dependencies.

The United States Department of Treasury has published two different model IGAs. Under Model 1, financial institutions in a partner country report information about USA accounts to their local tax authority. That tax authority then provides the information to the United States IRS. Under Model 2, a partner country agrees to lower any legal barriers to allow financial institutions in that country to report directly to the IRS. The table below sets out the approach by the governments of the other jurisdictions in which Apple by operates.

The actions and laws of USA is NOT unique worldwide. For example, in Dec. 2013, French court gives go ahead for Hollande's 75% tax: Plans for rate on earnings over one million euros. Now companies will have to pay 75 percent tax on all annual salaries exceeding one million euros, the equivalent of £ 830 000. It has already led to entrepreneurs and celebrities leaving France, but Mr Hollande is determined to see the policy implemented. France is hotly argue this tax will lead to mass exodus of celebrities and businesses. For example, the boss of LVMH flee to neighboring country-Belgium.

The Council originally rejected the measure in March, saying that it was against the law to levy taxes on individuals, rather than on households. But in a ruling published, the council said a reformulated tax "conforms with (France's) constitution". Employers will now have to pay 50 per cent income tax on salaries they pay above 1m, or £ 830 000. Social charges will bring the effective rate up to 75 per cent. The tax will apply for incomes paid this year, 2013, and in 2014. Mr Hollande has admitted that he "dislikes the rich", but insisted his new tax did not aim "to punish" them. He said he hoped it will encourage companies to lower executive pay during tough economic times. But it comes as the French economy veers from crisis to crisis - all of them blamed on Mr Hollande's mismanagement.

Reference: http://www.applebyglobal.com/footer/fatca.aspx

Hollande's 75% tax. http: //www. dailymail. co. uk/news/article-2530798/French-court-gives-ahead-Hollandes-75-tax-Plans-rate-earnings-one-million-euros-lead-mass-exodus-celebrities-businesses. html

Discussion:

1. IMF once pointed out 50% world trade is transited through tax heaven. Please discuss the role of tax heaven intax-avoidance, money-laundry etc.

2. How the 75% tax will accelerate themass exodus of celebrities and businesses out of France? Why President Hollande insisted this reform?

3. Please discuss global anti-corruption framework as well as that in China.

Extended Reading:

1. FCPA (Foreign Corrupt Practices Act) provisions and evolution (1977, 1988, 1994, 1998)

2. UN Global Compact (2002)

3. OECD Convention on Combating Bribery of Foreign Public Officials in International business (1993)

4. United Nations Convention against Corruption (UNCAC) (2005)《联合国反贪公约》

5. Canadian Corruption of Foreign Public Officials Act (CFPOA)

6. UK Bribery Act (2010)

7. Brazil Clean Company Act (2014)

8. Foreign Account Tax Compliance Act (FATCA) 2014 (肥猫法)

9. Law of the People's Republic of China on Anti-money Laundering《中华人民共和国反洗钱法》(2006)

10. Financial Institutions Anti Money Laundering Regulations《金融机构反洗钱规定》

11. Financial Institutions of Large Value and Suspicious Transactions Reporting Management Approach《金融机构大额交易和可疑交易报告管理办法》(2007);

12.

Read *Countering Small Bribes* by Transparency International and discuss how to handle small bribes in international business.

Case: Monsato: GMO Monopoly Worldwide

Monsato (美国孟山都公司) is world GMO (gene-modified organism) monopoly, the company claimed itself as a sustainable agriculture company Which deliver agricultural products that support farmers all around the world. The company focuse on empowering farmers—large and small—to produce more from their land while conserving more of our world's natural resources such as water and energy. Through its leading seed brands in crops like corn, cotton, oilseeds and fruits and vegetables, Monsato produce leading in-the-seed trait technologies for farmers, which are aimed at protecting their yield, supporting their on-farm efficiency and reducing their on-farm costs. Monsato claimed itself strive to make our products available to farmers throughout the world by broadly licensing our seed and trait technologies to other companies. In addition to seeds and traits business, Monsato also manufacture Roundup and other herbicides used by farmers, consumers and lawn-and-garden professionals.

There's nothing Monsato is leaving untouched: the mustard, the okra, the bringe oil, the rice, the cauliflower. Once they have established the norm: that seed can be owned as their property, royalties can be collected. We will depend on them for every seed we grow of every crop we grow. If they control seed, they control food, they know it - it's strategic. It's more powerful than bombs. It's more powerful than guns.

This is the best way to control the populations of the world. The story starts in the White House, where Monsanto often got its way by exerting disproportionate influence over policymakers via the "revolving door". One example is Michael Taylor, who worked for Monsanto as an attorney before being appointed as deputy commissioner of the US Food and Drug Administration (FDA) in 1991. While at the FDA, the authority that deals with all US food approvals, Taylor made crucial decisions that led to the approval of GE foods and crops. Then he returned to Monsanto, becoming the company's vice president for public policy.

Thanks to these intimate links between Monsanto and government agencies, the US adopted GE foods and crops without proper testing, without consumer labeling and in spite of serious questions hanging over their safety. Not coincidentally, Monsanto supplies 90 percent of the GE seeds used by the US market.

Monsanto's long arm stretched so far that, in the early nineties, the US Food and Drugs Agency even ignored warnings of their own scientists, who were cautioning that GE crops could cause negative health effects. Other tactics the company uses to stifle concerns about their products include misleading advertising, bribery and concealing scientific evidence.

Reference: http://topdocumentaryfilms.com/the-world-according-to-monsanto/

Case: Coca-Cola Has Donated More Than $ 3.2 Million to Defeat GMO Labeling: Boycott the Soda Empire (2014)

Coca-Cola and its products are becoming boycotted garbage due to the growing public awareness concerning companies who are supporting the defeat of GMO labeling. Now, you can tell this mega-corporation that while the $ 3.2 million spent to help defeat Proposition 37 in California and I-522 in Washington may have worked before, the organization is about to lose millions more in public product support. We have a right to know what is in our food, and nothing will stop the grassroots efforts to rid the world of GMO for good.

People all over the globe are boycotting Coca-Cola, Honest Tea, Odwalla, Zico, Peace Tea, and Vitamin Water until they stop supporting companies like Dow and Monsanto. Many people have stopped drinking Coke itself since it amounts to little more than sugar-water, but their other brands hang in the balance, too, as consumers stand ready to do what it takes to defeat the Grocery Manufacturer's Association (GMA) and biotech. Last year alone, Coca-Cola secretly spent more than $ 1.5 million through a slush fund to help defeat GMO labeling. They, along with companies like Kraft, Pepsi, General Mills, and others are keeping Americans poisoned on genetically modified foods and the herbicides and pesticides required to grow them.

Coca-Cola and other soda manufacturers don't want GMO labeling to pass because they use GMO sugar-beets to help sweeten their best-selling products, among other GMO crops.

GMO Labeling Ballot Initiative (I-522) in Washington could have given citizens the right to know, mandating clear labeling of genetically engineered ingredients on food packages. Numerous companies have spent hundreds or thousands and millions of dollars to fight this GMO labeling bill. Coca cola was among them at $ 1 047 000. Monsanto contributed $ 4 834 000.

Large food and seed corporations sunk over $ 46 million into the fight to defeat Proposition 37 in California alone, which would have required food companies to list genetically modified ingredients on the labels of its products sold in retail stores. It would have also prevented the labeling of GMO foods as "natural". Coca-cola spent $ 1 700 000 to defeat GMO labeling in the state, while Monsanto shelled out $ 7 100 000. And now, companies will be suing Vermont over the state's GMO labeling law, despite the fact that demanding GMO labeling is NOT unconstitutional.

Since the GMA has threatened even to take Vermont to court over their recent GMO labeling win, it behooves us all to tell Coca-Cola and their CEO, Muhtar Kent, we've had enough! Aside from boycotting the company's products, you can also sign a petition telling Coke just what you plan to do at Food Democracy Now. Tell Coke to Kiss Monsanto Goodbye!

Reference: http://naturalsociety.com/coca-cola-donated-3-2-million-defeat-gmo-labeling/

Discussion:

1. In 2002, China became the first sovereignty state which import GMO without setting a safety-control and detection period. What's more, China is the only country worldwide to carry GMO practices on her stale food grain, such as rice, corn, cotton, potato. How do you look at this unique phenomenon?

Online Practice and Extended Reading:

1. Visit the company's homepage: www.monsanto.com

2. Watch Documentary online:

http://www.tudou.com/programs/view/6AH_EFMgpMs/孟山都公司眼中的世界

Discussion:

1. Social accountability covers 9 areas: Child Labor, Forced or Compulsory Labor, Health & Safety, Freedom of Association & Right to Collective Bargaining, Discrimination, Disciplinary Practices, Working Hours, Remuneration, Management Systems. Please tell how these standards can protect the basic human rights of workers.

2. TNCs from developed countries always carry out dual-standard of social Accountability worldwide, that is in developed countries, they comply strictly with SA8000, but in developing countries, that just ignore SA8000. How do you look at this strange phenomenon ?

Online Practices and Extended Reading:

1. Visit the homepage of www.ilo.org (国际劳工组织).

2. Visit the homepage of Social Accountability International (SAI): www.sa-intl.org.

3. Please read provisions of SA8000 (Social Accountability 8000): 2014.

The SA8000 Standard is one of the world's first auditable social certification standards for decent workplaces, across all industrial sectors. It is based on the UN Declaration of Human Rights, conventions of the ILO, UN and national law. Those seeking to comply with SA8000 have adopted policies and procedures that protect the basic human rights of workers.

4. Please compare 2008 Standard and SA8000 2014 Standard.

5. Visit the homepage of ISO, the International Organization for Standardization: www.iso.org. Click ISO26000. Read Provisions of ISO26000《社会责任指南》(2012).

· ISO, the International Organization for Standardization, launched an International Standard providing guidelines for social responsibility (SR) named ISO 26000 or simply ISO SR. It was released on 1 November 2010. Its goal is to contribute to global sustainable development, by encouraging business and other organizations to practice social responsibility to improve their impacts on their workers, their natural environments and their communities.

6. Search internet the following guidelines and principles:

· OECD Guidelines for Multinational Enterprises (1976)

· OECD Principles of Corporate Governance (1998, 2004)

· UN Global Compact (2002)

Case: Over Two Million UK Public Sector Workers Strike (2011)

December 2, 2011, over two million UK public sector workers strike By Julie Hyland 01 Dec 2011. Over two million public sector workers took part yesterday in a 24-hour strike against the Conservative/Liberal Democrat government's attack on their pensions. The largest national walk-out for more than 30 years involved members of 37 unions in an action backed by the Trades Union Congress (TUC). They included teachers, health workers, civil servants and workers in local authorities and other areas of social provision, angered at the coalition's plans to make public service employees pay more, and work longer for lower pensions on retirement.

Figure 1. Annual day off in EU

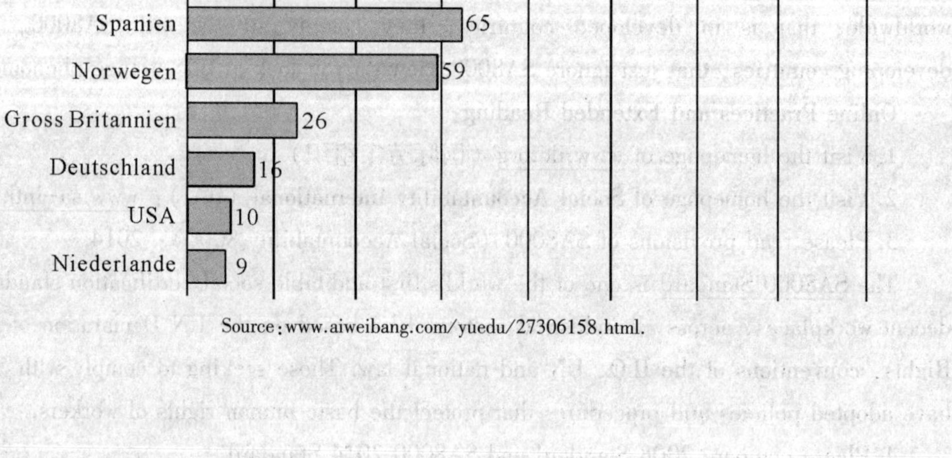

Source: www.aiweibang.com/yuedu/27306158.html.

Figure2. Annual strike days in EU

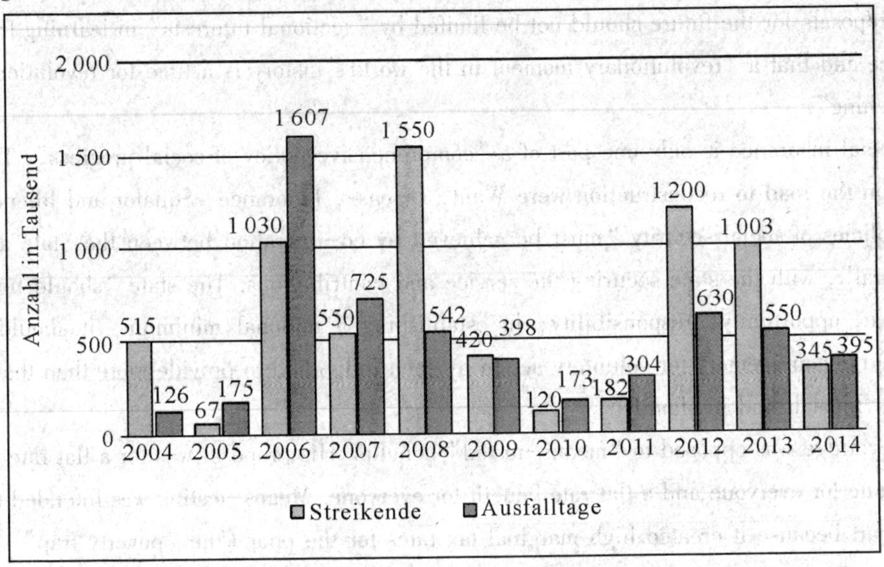

Source: www.aiweibang.com/yuedu/27306158.html.

On-line Practices:

1. Search how the right of strike evolved in UK, France and USA during the last century?

2. Search UN Global Compact (2002), Principle 3: the freedom of association and the effective recognition of the right to collective bargaining.

Discussion:

1. Discuss how the freedom of association and the effective recognition of the right to collective bargaining affect the labor practices in UK and other western states.

2. The 1982 Constitution in China deprive the strike right in China, while the 1975 and 1978 constitution empowered the Chinese the right of strike. Please discuss the evolve of strike rights in China.

Extended Reading:

William Beveridge Report (1941): Founder of Modern Social Welfare System

The Beveridge Report, officially entitled Social Insurance and Allied Services, was an influential document in the founding of the welfare state in the United Kingdom which was published in November 1942. It was chaired by the Liberal economist William Beveridge, who identified five "Giant Evils" in society: Squalor, Ignorance, Want, Idleness, and Disease, and went on to propose widespread reform to the system of social welfare to address these. The Report came in the midst of war, and promised a reward for the sacrifices undertaken by everyone. Highly popular with the public, the report formed the basis for the post-war reforms known as the Welfare State, which include the expansion of National Insurance and the creation of the National Health Service. The report was printed by Alabaster Passmore & Sons Limited which kept their factory in Maidstone busy when there was very little other printing work available.

The Report offered three guiding principles to its recommendations:

Proposals for the future should not be limited by "sectional interests" in learning from experience and that a "revolutionary moment in the world's history is a time for revolutions, not for patching".

Social insurance is only one part of a "comprehensive policy of social progress". The five giants on the road to reconstruction were Want, Disease, Ignorance, Squalor and Idleness.

Policies of social security "must be achieved by co-operation between the State and the individual", with the state securing the service and contributions. The state "should not stifle incentive, opportunity, responsibility; in establishing a national minimum, it should leave room and encouragement for voluntary action by each individual to provide more than that minimum for himself and his family".

Beveridge was opposed to "means-tested" benefits. His proposal was for a flat rate contribution rate for everyone and a flat rate benefit for everyone. Means-testing was intended to play a tiny part because it created high marginal tax rates for the poor (the "poverty trap").

Reaction

Inside the Cabinet, there was debate, instigated byBrendan Bracken, on 16 November 1942 over whether to publish the Report as a White Paper at that time. The Chancellor of the Exchequer, Sir Kingsley Wood, said that it involved "an impracticable financial commitment" and that publication should therefore be postponed. However, the Cabinet decided on 26 November to publish it on 2 December.

The Ministry of Information Home Intelligence found that the Report had been "welcomed with almost universal approval by people of all shades of opinion and by all sections of the community" and seen as "the first real attempt to put into practice the talk about a new world". In a sample taken in the fortnight after the Report's publication, the British Institute of Public Opinion found that 95% of the public had heard of the Report and that there was "great interest in it", but criticism that old age pensions were not high enough. They also found that "there was overwhelming agreement that the plan should be put into effect".

The Times said of the Report: "a momentous document which should and must exercise a profound and immediate influence on the direction of social change in Britain". The Manchester Guardian called it "a big and fine thing". The Daily Telegraph said it was a consummation of the revolution begun by David Lloyd George in 1911. The Archbishop of Canterbury, William Temple, said it was "the first time anyone had set out to embody the whole spirit of the Christian ethic in an Act of Parliament".

There was a planned debate in Parliament on the Report for February 1943 so the Cabinet appointed the Lord President of the Council, Sir John Anderson, to chair a committee to consider the Report and to set out the government's line in the Commons debate. In the Commons debate the government announced they would not implement the Report immediately. The Tory Reform Committee, consisting of 45 Conservative MPs, demanded the founding of a Ministry of

Social Security immediately. At the division at the end of the debate, 97 Labour MPs, 11 Independents, 9 Liberals, 3 Independent Labour Party MPs and 1 Communist voted against the government. A Ministry of Information Home Intelligence report found that after the debate the left-wing section of the public were disappointed but that "an approving minority" thought that the government was correct in waiting until the post-war financial situation were known before making a decision. An opinion poll by the British Institute of Public Opinion found that 29% were satisfied with the government's attitude to the Report; 47% were dissatisfied and 24% "don't knows".

Winston Churchill gave a broadcast on 21 March 1943 entitled "After the War", where he warned the public not to impose "great new expenditure on the State without any relation to the circumstances which might prevail at the time" and said there would be "a four-year plan" of post-war reconstruction "to cover five or six large measures of a practical character" which would be put to the electorate after the war and implemented by a new government. These measures were "national compulsory insurance for all classes for all purposes from the cradle to the grave"; the abolition of unemployment by government policies which would "exercise a balancing influence upon development which can be turned on or off as circumstances require"; "a broadening field for state ownership and enterprise"; new housing; major reforms to education; largely expanded health and welfare services. Churchill's commitment to creating a welfare state was limited and he and the Conservative Party opposed much of the implementation of the Beveridge Report, including voting against the founding of the NHS.

The Labour Party won the 1945 general election on a platform that promised to address what the Beveridge report called "the five giant evils" of society: Want, Disease, Ignorance, Squalor, and Idleness. Beveridge's recommendation were implemented through a series of acts of parliament (namely the National Insurance Act, the National Assistance Act and the National Health Service Act), founding the modern welfare state. Labour deviated somewhat from Beveridge in the role the state would play in the provision of key services. Labour leaders opposed Beveridge's idea of a National Health Service run through local health centres and regional hospital administrations, preferring a state-run body. Beveridge complained about the opposition of Labour leaders, including that of Ernest Bevin: "For Ernest Bevin, with his trade-union background of unskilled workers... social insurance was less important than bargaining about wages." Bevin derided the Beveridge Report as a "Social Ambulance Scheme" and followed the Coalition Government's view that it should not be implemented until the end of the war (he was furious in February 1943 when a large number of Labour back-benchers ignored their leaders and voted against delay in implementing Beveridge).

Wartime changes

The war years saw great improvements in working conditions and welfare provisions, which paved the way for the postwar welfare state. Infant, child, and maternity services were expanded, while the Official Food Policy Committee (chaired by the deputy PM and Labour leader-

Clement Attlee) approved grants of fuel and subsidised milk to mothers and to children under the age of five in June 1940. A month later, the Board of Education decided that free school meals should become more widely available. By February 1945, 73% of children received milk in school, compared with 50% in July 1940. Free vaccination against diphtheria was also provided for children at school. In addition, the Town and Country Planning Act 1944 gave consideration to those areas damaged in bombing raids and enabled local authorities to clear slums, while the Housing (Temporary Accommodation) Act passed that same year made £ 150 million available for the construction of temporary dwellings.

To improve conditions for elderly persons, supplementary pensions were introduced in 1940, and in 1943, there were further improvements in rates and conditions for those in receipt of supplementary pensions and unemployment assistance. Food prices were stabilised in December 1939, initially as temporary measure, but made permanent in August 1940, while both milk and meals were provided at subsidised prices, or free in those cases of real need.

In July 1940, increased Treasury grants led to an improvement in the supply of milks and meals in schools, with the number of meals taken doubled within a year and increased school milk by 50%. By 1945, roughly 33% of all children ate at school compared with just 3.3% (one in thirty) in 1940, while those taking milk increased from about 50% to roughly 75%. In 1940, a national milk scheme was launched, which provided a pint of milk at about half price for all children under the age of five, and for expectant or nursing mothers. The take-up rate was such that, by 1944, 95% of those eligible had participated in the scheme. The government's general food policy that priority groups like young children and mothers were not just entitled to essentials like milk, but actually received supplies as well. Evacuation during the course of the war also revealed, to more prosperous Britons, the extent of deprivation in society. As noted by one historian, evacuation became "the most important subject in the social history of the war because it revealed, to the whole people, the black spots in its social life."

An Emergency Hospital Service was introduced, which provided free treatment to casualties (a definition which included war evacuees), while rationing led to significant improvements in the diets of poor families. As noted by Richard Titmuss,

"The families in that third of the population ofBritain who, in 1938, were chronically undernourished, had their first adequate diet in 1940 and 1941... (after which) the incidence of deficiency diseases, and notably infant mortality, dropped dramatically."

Implementation:

The Labour Party eventually also adopted the Beveridge proposals, and after their victory in the 1945 general election, they proceeded to implement many social policies, which became known as the Welfare State. These included the Family Allowances Act 1945, National Insurance (Industrial Injuries) Act 1946, National Insurance Act 1946, National Health Service Act 1946, Pensions (Increase) Act 1947, Landlord and Tenant (Rent Control) Act 1949, National Insurance (Industrial Injuries) Act 1948, National Insurance Act 1949.

Reference: https://en.wikipedia.org/wiki/Beveridge_Report

Discussion:

There is a saying that the PIGS Crisis (Portugal, Italy, Ireland, Greece and Spain &their sovereignty debt crisis) is cause by their luxury welfare system and the states can't afford and their welfare sates can't be sustainable. What is your opinion?

Case: Thailand's $ 7 Billion Global Seafood Industry Runs on Brutal Slave Labor (2014)

BANGKOK — For years, it was a poorly kept secret. Thailand's fishing industry — a key supplier to the US — is entangled in barbaric slavery. Today, slave labor on Thai trawlers is no longer a secret. It's a worldwide scandal.

Wave after wave of damning investigations — previously by *GlobalPost*, most recently by *The Guardian* — have helped reveal an underground trade in which men are press-ganged into toiling on the seas for zero pay. Smuggled from poor villages in Myanmar or Cambodia, with promises of jobs on land, men and teen boys are instead forced onto Thai-owned boats plying distant waters. Quitting is forbidden. Disobedience is punished with beatings, dismemberment and worse.

Many of these migrants — and the Thai boatmen who lord over them — have told *GlobalPost* that murder on Thai trawlers is practically routine. As one Thai crewman explained: "I saw an entire foreign crew shot dead... The boss didn't want to pay up so he lined them up on the side of the boat and shot them one by one."

This practice's horrors have become so well known that — after years of giving Thailand a pass — the US may announce sanctions against the Southeast Asian nation this week. The implications could be huge for Thailand's $ 7 billion global seafood industry. Thailand is America's second-largest seafood supplier thanks in large part to Western appetites for cheap shrimp and fish sticks.

But there is one commodity churned out by this industry that's notoriously reliant on forcedlabor. It's called "trash fish" — and it's as unpleasant as it sounds. Trash fish doesn't refer to a single species. It's a catch-all term for two types of wild-caught seafood: species that are unpalatable (to human tongues, at least) and species that would grow into big, tasty fish if nets had not snared them so young. Trash fish are only valuable once they're ground to a mush used to produce livestock feed, pet chow, fish oil and cheap processed food. The link between trash fish and forced labor is clear. The accounts of escaped slaves indicate that victims invariably work on Thai-owned trawlers, small vessels that travel vast distances to dredge trash fish in giant nets. Southeast Asia's seas are so overfished that high-value species are increasingly rare. The scarcity of quality fish forces trawler captains to scour for loads and loads of trash fish — a grueling, labor-intensive chore.

"There is great pressure to drive down costs," said Steve Trent, executive director of the

London-based Environmental Justice Foundation, which has conducted extensive investigations into forced labor on Thai trawlers. "In some people's minds, that's practically legitimized the use of slave labor." "The fisheries are out of control," Trent said. "There is no effective management. In a relatively short time, since the industrial trawlers were introduced to the region, you've had a more than 90 percent decline in catch. They're crumbling beneath the weight of this mismanagement."

Much of the supply chain from trawler net to supermarket is simply not monitored or properly policed. By the time slavery-tainted fish reaches the shore, the origins have been obscured by a series of fishmongers and middlemen. The system is so murky that seafood companies can't honestly assert that their trash fish purchases are slavery free.

"They're claimed they don't know. Or they're preferred to look the other way," Trent said. "But now you have clear evidence of abuse in the production of trash fish... and you cannot be sure you don't have something on your shelves that does not have slavery or forced labor in its production."

Here are three items reliant on trash fish that you may find in your pantry or freezer: Shrimp: Thailand is the world's largest shrimp exporter and and America's largest foreign shrimp supplier. The shrimp aren't directly farmed using forced labor. But shrimp are often fed the mushed-up sea life collected on slave boats. "That has been proven beyond any reasonable doubt," Trent said. *The Guardian* has directly implicated the planet's largest shrimp exporter — a massive Thailand-based conglomerate called CP Foods — in feeding slave-caught trash fish to shrimp. CP Foods has long sold shrimp to Walmart and Costco as well as Tesco, a UK-headquartered superstore chain, and France's Carrefour. So far, only Carrefour has stopped buying shrimp from CP Foods following *The Guardian's* expose.

Dog and cat food: Ground-up trash fish are a common ingredient in pet food. No investigation has linked a particular pet chow factory to forced labor but "it's wholly reasonable to expect that trash fish may be entering supply chains producing cat food and dog food," Trent said.

Last year, $ 171 million worth of dog and cat food entered the US from Thailand, according to the United States Department of Agriculture. When it comes to dog and cat food in "sealed in airtight containers" — which typically means wet pet food — Thailand is America's top foreign supplier. Fish sauce: Trash fish is a key ingredient in fish sauce — a savory, amber-colored liquid. In many Asian kitchens, it's an ingredient no less crucial than salt in western kitchens. In the US, Thai fish sauce rules 85 percent of the market. Last year, according the US government statistics, Americans consumed more than 35 million pounds of Thai-produced fish sauce. That's enough to feed two ounces of fish sauce to every American man, woman and child. Fish oil pills: A popular source of Omega 3 fatty acids, fish oil pills are sometimes produced with trash fish. Mackerel and sardines are common species used to make the pills. They're also common species caught by slaves on Thai trawlers. The Environmental

Justice Foundation has looked into links between slave-caught fish and factories and will "examine them further," Trent said. "I don't think people in the major consumer markets want to be eating a health product produced by slaves."

Reference: http: //www. businessinsider. com/thailands - seafood - industry - slave - labor-2014-6

Discussion:

According to the Principle 4 of UN Global Compact (2002): it says " the elimination of all forms of forced and compulsory labour". But why such slave labor still exist in Thailand?

PART THREE
The Global Trade and Investment Environment

CHAPTER 5
International Trade Theory

At the end of this chapter, you should be able to:

· Understand how the trade theory answers the motivation, patter and benefits-sharing;

· Be familiar with theclassical and new trade theories;

· Understand how the various trade theories' implication for business practices.

Case: New Mercantilism?

Mercantilism has had a "good press" in recent decades, in contrast to 19th-century opinion. In the days of Adam Smith and the classical economists, mercantilism was properly regarded as a blend of economic fallacy and state creation of special privilege. But in our century, the general view of mercantilism has changed drastically.

Keynesians hail mercantilists as prefiguring their own economic insights; Marxists hail mercantilism as a "progressive" step in the historical development of capitalism; socialists and interventionists salute mercantilism as anticipating modern state building and central planning.

Thus, a policy of favoring exports and penalizing imports had two important practical effects. These policies are in very many ways much closer to a mercantilist view of economic development than they are to the classic free-market view.

Reference: Murray N. Rothbard. Mercantilism: A Lesson for ourt times? http://mises.org/daily/4304; http://www.hks.harvard.edu/news-events/news/news-archive/chinese-good-or-bad

Discussion:

1. Mercantilism and Neo-mercantilism, similarity and differences.

2. Chinese economy is rooted in three engineers: namely investment, consumption and export. But recently, China not only accumulate huge surplus and reserves, but also become No. 1target of trade protectionism worldwide. How do you look at the fact that China in fact has high degree of foreign trade dependence?

Extended Reading: Washington Consensus (1989) VS Beijing Consensus (2009)

· The term Washington Consensus was coined in 1989 by English economist John Williamson to refer to a set of 10 relatively specific economic policy prescriptions that he considered constituted the "standard" reform package promoted for crisis-wracked developing countries by Washington, D. C. -based institutions such as the International Monetary Fund

(IMF), World Bank, and the US Treasury Department. The prescriptions encompassed policies in such areas as macroeconomic stabilization, economic opening with respect to both trade and investment, and the expansion of market forces within the domestic economy.

· The Beijing Consensus (also sometimes called the "China Model" or "Chinese Economic Model" is a term that refers to the political and especially economic policies of the People's Republic of China that began after the rehabilitation of Deng Xiaoping (1976) and are thought to have contributed to China's eightfold growth in gross national product over two decades. The phrase "Beijing Consensus" was coined by Joshua Cooper Ramo to pose China's economic development model as an alternative — especially for developing countries — to the Washington Consensus of market-friendly policies promoted by the IMF, World Bank and U. S. Treasury.

Discussion:

The approach of individual negotiating countries, both in industrialized and developing, has been to press for trade liberation in areas where their own comparative competitive advantages are the strongest, and to resist liberalization in areas where they are less competitive and fear that imports would replace domestic production.

——Jarl Hagelstam

A Director at the Finnish Ministry of Finance. *Mercantilism Still Influences Practical Trade Policy at the End of* 20*th Century*. Journal of World Trade, 1991, pp. 95-105.

Case: Financial Arbitrage Via Hong Kong/Mainland China Trade Is Expanding (2016)

The unusually large divergence of trade data between Hong Kong and the mainland indicates the use of trade channel for financial arbitrages might have expanded last month, says a research report by ANZ.

China's customs data indicated a surge in mainland's exports to and imports from Hong Kong by 11% and 64% year-on-year, respectively.

Hong Kong's statistics showed that Hong Kong's exports to mainland rose only 0.9% year-on-year, while imports from the mainland contracted 1.0%.

While a statistical discrepancy between trade data has always existed, Hong Kong's imports from the mainland in December was HK $ 183.7 billion (US $ 23.7 billion).

It is 48% lower than Mainland China's exports to Hong Kong released by China's customs (US $ 46.0 billion), but much higher than an average of around 24% during January to November in 2015, meaning such arbitrage activities may have picked up pace.

Given the spread between onshore CNY and offshore CNH, which widened to as much as over 900 basis points in December, exporters and importers may have moved funds across the border via trading with offshore affiliates.

By blowing up trade figures, traders may have potentially received a larger foreign exchange quota to move funds abroad.

Chinese authorities have reportedly tightened measures to curb capital outflows recently, including tightening cross-border RMB lending and suspension of foreign exchange trading for several foreign banks.

It is critical for the authorities to re-establish credibility and prevent the currency from weakening from certain threshold level.

China's capital market should be opened wider for foreign participation so as to encourage capital inflow, leading to two-way capital flows to dissipate RMB's one-way depreciation expectation, suggests the report.

FIGURE 1. HONG KONG-MAINLAND CHINA TRADE GAP

Reference: http://www.livemint.com/Money/Mv5oAfZAGjcSw0s0J3YmiP/Wider-China-Hong-Kong-anomaly-revives-fake-trade-doubt.html

http://www.chinamoneynetwork.com/2016/01/26/financial-arbitrage-via-hong-kong-china-trade-is-expanding

Exercises:

1. Please investigate and explore the up-to-date arbitrage practices between Mainland China and Hong Kong.

2. Please define the role of the Bonded Areas, Free Trade Zones and Hong Kong SAR in the interest arbitrage, exchange arbitrage and tax arbitrage practices. Could you stipulate some policy measures to monitor and regulate such practices.

CHAPTER 6
The Political Economy of International Trade

At the end of this chapter, you should be able to:

· Discuss free trade and fair trade argument;

· Understand the maintrade polices (tariff and non-tariff barriers);

· Understand why government prefer the intervention and the argument;

· Learn subsidy and quota in details;

· Discuss the "trade barriers" implication for business practices worldwide.

Case: Zero-Tariff Plan by USA (2002)

In Dec. 2002, USA proposed a fantastic planwhich is called "Zero-Tariff", the main idea is that by the year of 2015, all the member states of WTO will eliminate its tariff on all imported consumable goods and industrial goods.

But the reality is that the average tariff for such products in USA is about 2%, the average tariff level is about 3.3% of OECD member states (the rich club). But the vast majority of the world, the huge number developing countries, their average is 13% and heavily rely on duty revenues, just can't match that of USA. That is why from the very beginning, Zero-tariff plan suffered criticism.

Discussion:

1. Discuss the hypercritical of the so-called zero-trariff plan.

Online Practices:

1. Visit the homepage of US Customs and Border Protection (CBP, 美国海关总署) www.cbp.gov. learn more customs practices.

2. Please study in details USHTS (Harmonized Tariff Schedule of US, 美国海关关税税则). There are 99 chapters in USHTS.

3. When importing a product intoUSA, the USHTS code is different, then the corresponding tariff and duty are different. For example, a toy (玩具) and a figure (人偶玩具) are different, the former applied much lower tax. Please use X-Man (X 战警) as an example, and see how CBP classify such products, a toy or a figure?

Case: Sino-African Trade &Investment Boom

In recent years, China-Africa trade development has maintained comparatively rapid momentum. In 2009, China became Africa's No. 1 trade partner. In the following two years, the scale of China-Africa trade expanded rapidly. In 2012, the total volume of China-Africa trade reached US $ 198. 49 billion, a year-on-year growth of 19. 3%. Of this, US $ 85. 319 billion consisted of China's exports to Africa, up 16. 7%, and US $ 113. 171 billion was contributed by China's imports from Africa, up 21. 4%. Total China-Africa trade volume, China's export volume to Africa and China's import volume from Africa all reached new highs.

From 2000 to 2012, the proportion of China-Africa trade volume as a part of China's total foreign trade volume increased from 2. 23% to 5. 13%; the proportion consisting of China's imports from Africa up from 2. 47% to 6. 23%, and that of China's exports to Africa from 2. 02% to 4. 16%. On the African side, the changes are even more remarkable. From 2000 to 2012, the proportion of China-Africa trade volume as a part of Africa's total foreign trade volume increased from 3. 82% to 16. 13%: the proportion contributed by Africa's exports to China up from 3. 76% to 18. 07%, and that by Africa's imports from China from 3. 88% to 14. 11%.

Since 2009, Africa has seen a decrease of foreign direct investment, but an accelerated growth of direct investment from China during this same period. From 2009 to 2012, China's direct investment in Africa increased from US $ 1. 44 billion to US $ 2. 52 billion, with an annual growth rate of 20. 5%. Over the same period, China's accumulative direct investment in Africa increased from US $ 9. 33 billion to US $ 21. 23 billion, 2. 3 times the 2009 figure. The rapid growth of China's direct investment in Africa is indicative of Africa's development potential and investment appeal, and also points to the mutually beneficial nature of China-Africa cooperation.

Discussion and online practices:

1. In march 2013, Chairman Xi Jinping visited Africa and brought huge investment in Africa. How do you look at the new role of Africa to Chinese development?

2. Historically, African community are very friendly with Chinese. But with recent boom of trade andinvestment between China and Africa, conflicts is soaring. Could you analyze this new phenomena and give some reasons as well as propose some measures to reduce conflicts ? For example, help the local community to sustainable development etc.

3. Visit China in Africa www.chinainafrica.co.uk, learn more info about Sino-Africa trade and investment.

Reference: China-Africa Economic and Trade Cooperation (2013). http://news.xinhuanet.com/english/china/2013-08/29/c_132673093_2.htm

Case: Farmers Defend Controversial EU Subsidies (2010-2013)

The EU's complex and costly system of farm subsidies is under review in Dec. 2010 the

European Commission present its reform plans.

The EU's Common Agricultural Policy (CAP) cost the biggest EU budget item - about 47% of total in 2010. Average annual subsidy per farm: 12 200 euros (£ 10 374). France is biggest beneficiary. France - the EU's biggest food producer - does not want farm subsidies to be cut, unless global rivals like the US also agree to cut their subsidies. But the UK wants far-reaching reform of the EU's Common Agricultural Policy (CAP), with less spent on food production and more on the environment.

In the past 40 years rural EU has seen seismic change. It now accounts for less than 3% of the whole workforce. In France, the number of farms has plunged from two million in 1960 to around 650 000 today. With globalisation, food producers and wholesalers can afford to shop around, driving the prices down. It means farmers cannot cover the costs of producing their cereal, wheat, or milk. Farmers across Europe receives CAP money each year.

But in 2012, EU plans for "green" farm-subsidy rules will reduce European food production and are likely to harm the environment. EU wants 30% of farm subsidies to be conditional on whether recipient farms have met certain environmental standards, a policy it has branded "greening" the CAP. Under the proposals, farmers will need to grow at least three different crops, leave 7% of their land fallow and ensure that permanent pasture is maintained on their land. It is a nonsense to think that farmers from Finland to Sicily should be tied to the same narrow prescriptive rules. One-size-fits all regulation cannot work across the range of environments found in Europe.

Reference: Farmers defend controversial EU subsidies. http://www.bbc.com/news/world-europe-11476656. 18 October 2010.

MPs criticise "green" EU farm-subsidy conditions. http://www.bbc.com/news/uk-politics-18263737 June 2012.

Discussion:

1. Why EU offer huge subsidy to farmers?

2. Please discuss how subsidyencourage over-production, inefficiency and reduced trade?

3. Please talk about different agricultural subsidy policies, for example, EU, Japan and USA offered huge subsidy to farmers. Could you compare their subsidy policy?

Extended Reading: Is JP Morgan a Farmer?

-How the nation's biggest banks use the little-covered House Agriculture Committee to gut regulations

Imagine you're a finance lobbyist and want to move deregulation and other industry-friendly policies through Congress. While you might think the House Financial Services Committee would be the logical place to do it — since it has jurisdiction over financial issues, naturally — what if there were a sneaky way to maneuver it through a far less scrutinized committee, so most people would have no idea what you were doing?

This is the story of how the world's largest banks came to love the House Agriculture Committee. In Washington, we often witness politicians forgetting the lessons of a year or five years or 10 years ago. It takes some special obliviousness to forget the lessons of Friday. Five days ago, Sen. Carl Levin, D-Mich., delivered a critical rcport and heldan explosive hearing detailing the "London Whale" trades, made by a JP Morgan Chase satellite office in London. As you may have read, these trades turned sour and led to a $ 6. 2 billion loss for the bank in a matter of weeks. More important, JP Morgan misled regulators about the nature of the trades, altered its internal processes to take on more risk, and then hid the losses by improperly mismarking the value on its balance sheet, pretending the shortfall was inconsequential to avoid oversight and present a positive financial picture to investors.

The Whale trades, which totaled $ 157 billion at their peak, are known to the industry as derivatives, massive bets on bets that present outsize risk to financial institutions and the broader economy. And of course, derivatives helped fuel the financial crisis of 2008. But less than a week after the Levin report, the House Agriculture Committee will hold amarkup session today on seven bills designed to gut derivatives regulations passed in the Dodd-Frank financial reform law. If the bills pass, practically every improper and illegal action that JP Morgan Chase took in the London Whale debacle would be either made legal or allowed to foster outside of regulatory oversight. It borders on unthinkable that lawmakers on both sides of the aisle would pick this moment to undermine derivatives rules, right when we get a case study in the dangers of bank misuse of derivatives. (As Bartlett Naylor of Public Citizen told Salon, "At least the NRA isn't proposing that all citizens should be allowed to own surface-to-air missiles in their homes.")

Reference: http://www.salon.com/2013/03/20/j_p_morgan_is_not_a_farmer/

Discussion:

How do America's biggest banks use the little-covered House Agriculture Committee to gut regulations?

Case: Esquel Search Import Quotas Worldwide

Based in Hong Kong, Esquel Group (www.esquel.com, 溢达集团) is the world largest manufacturer of men's cotton shirts. The annual output is 90 million yards, about 50 million shirts every year. There are 55 000 employees in 11 countries and in 2012 the 1 sales revues is 1. 2 Billion USD. Its customers include Polo Ralph Lauren, Tommy Hilfiger, Brooks Brothers, Hugo Boss, Nordstrom, Eddie Bauer, Abercrombie and Fitch.

Esquel owns factories worldwide, including China, Malaysia, Vietnam, Mauritius (毛里求斯) and Maldives (马尔代夫)... It is most shocking to see Mauritius and Maldives are the factory base for cotton shirt production. Since textile is most famous for its high labor-intensive and cheap labor/land seeking industry? Why Esquel prefer the two small islands as production bases.

The secret is QUOTA（配额）. As world No. 1 exporter of cotton shirts, Esquel already exhaust the quota of Hong Kong, Mainland China etc. That is why Esquel has to search worldwide for new quota and navigate around import quota. Even though Mauritius and Maldives are small islets and most expensive land/labor, plus remote international transportation, still the two islets are best choice of navigating import quota.

Import Quota

An import quota is a limit on the quantity of a good that can be produced abroad and sold domestically. It is a type of protectionist trade restriction that sets a physical limit on the quantity of a good that can be imported into a country in a given period of time. If a quota is put on a good, less of it is imported. Quotas, like other trade restrictions, are used to benefit the producers of a good in a domestic economy at the expense of all consumers of the good in that economy.

The primary goal of import quotas is to reduce imports and increase domestic production of a good, service, or activity, thus "protect" domestic production by restricting foreign competition. As the quantity of importing the good is restricted, the price of the imported good increases, thus encourages consumers to purchase more domestic products. In general, a quota is simply a legal quantity restriction placed on a good imported that is imposed by the domestic government.

Because the import quota prevents domestic consumers from buying an imported good, the supply of the good is no longer perfectly elastic at the world price. Instead, as long as the price of the good is above the world price, the license holders import as much as they are permitted, and the total supply of the good equals the domestic supply plus the quota amount. The price of the good adjusts to balance supply (domestic plus imported) and demand. The quota causes the price of the good to rise above the world price. The imported quantity demanded falls and the domestic quantity supplied rises. Thus, the import quota reduces the imports. Because the quota raises the domestic price above the world price, domestic sellers are better off, and domestic buyers are worse off. In addition, the license holders are better off because they make a profit from buying at the world price and selling at the higher domestic price. Thus, import quotas decrease consumer surplus while increasing producer surplus and license-holder surplus.

Reference: www.esquel.com. http://www.baidu.com/s?tn=91336890_hao_pg&ie=utf-8&bs=quotas&f=3&rsv_bp=1&wd=import++quotas&inputT=2922

Discussion:

Information concerning textile import quotas may be obtained from the CBP web, www.cbp.gov/xp/cgov/import/textiles_and_quotas/textile_status. Search the internet for more info and practice of textile import quotas.

Extended Reading: Multi Fibre Arrangement (MFA)

The Multi Fibre Arrangement (MFA) governed the world trade intextiles and garments from 1974 through 2004, imposing quotas on the amount developing countries could export to developed countries. It expired on 1 January 2005.

The MFA was introduced in 1974 as a short-term measure intended to allow developed countries to adjust to imports from the developing world. Developing countries have an absolute advantage in textile production because it is labor-intensive and they have low labor costs. According to a World Bank/International Monetary Fund (IMF) study, the system has cost the developing world 27 million jobs and $ 40 billion a year in lost exports.

At the General Agreement on Tariffs and Trade (GATT) Uruguay Round, it was decided to bring the textile trade under the jurisdiction of the World Trade Organization. The Agreement on Textiles and Clothing provided for the gradual dismantling of the quotas that existed under the MFA. This process was completed on 1 January 2005. However, large tariffs remain in place on many textile products.

Bangladesh was expected to suffer the most from the ending of the MFA, as it was expected to face more competition, particularly from China. However, this was NOT the case. It turns out that even in the face of other economic giants, Bangladesh's labor is "cheaper than anywhere else in the world". While some smaller factories were documented making pay cuts and layoffs, most downsizing was essentially speculative—the orders for goods kept coming even after the MFA expired. In fact, Bangladesh's exports increased in value by about $ 500 million in 2006. However, poorer countries within the developed world, such as Greece and Portugal, are expected to lose out.

During early 2005, textile and clothing exports from China to the West grew by 100% or more in many items, leading the US and EU to cite China's WTO accession agreement allowing them to restrict the rate of growth to 7.5% per year until 2008. In June, China agreed with the EU to limit the rate to 10% for 3 years. No such agreement was reached with the US, which imposed its own import growth quotas of 7.5% instead. When the EU announced their new quotas to replace the lapsed MFA, Chinese manufacturers accelerated their shipping of the goods intended for the European market. This used up a full year's quota almost immediately. As a result, 75 million items of imported Chinese garments were held in European ports in August 2005. A diplomatic resolution was reached at the beginning of September 2005 during Tony Blair's visit to China, putting an end to a situation the UK press had dubbed "Bra Wars".

Reference: http://en.wikipedia.org/wiki/Multi-Fiber_Agreement

Discussion:

The Multi Fibre Arrangement (MFA) governing world trade in textiles and garments from 1974 through 2004, imposing quotas and t expired on 1 January 2005. But the textile and garments industrials still suffer Safegaurd (特保) from USA; Together the EU announced their new quotas to replace the lapsed MFA. How do you look at the new dilemma faced by Chinese companies?

CHAPTER 7
Foreign Direct Investment

At the end of this chapter, you should be able to:

· FDI, Greenfield, M&A;

· Pro and cons of FDI and its argumentworldwide;

· Understand the basic theories of FDI;

· Evaluate the political ideology of various governments to FDI;

· Government policy instruments.

Case: From JV to Whole-Owned Subsidiary (2002)

Since China adopted open-an-reform policy in 1978, foreign capital flooded in China. the inflow FDI (Foreign Direct Investment) into China is 127 Billion USA (the year of 2013), ranking No. 2 worldwide, just after USA. In early times, TNCs prefer Joint Venture (JV) as best entry mode into China. Because JV enjoys many benefits and windfalls.

A joint venture is a business agreement in which the parties agree to develop for a finite time, a new entity and new assets by contributing equity. They exercise control over the enterprise and consequently share revenues, expenses and assets. There are other types of companies such as JV limited by guarantee, joint ventures limited by guarantee with partners holding shares.

Benefits of joint venture include: it would give the company relatively low cost access to the foreign market; foreign government offers tax concessions to the company for bring FDI into the country, such a foreign partner could assist with the issues relating to marketing, cultural and language and dealing with government restrictions and bureaucracy; joint venture arrangement eliminates the need to source new premises and gives easier access to foreign capital markets which would reduce any foreign currency risks.

But the story changed since 2002. Just after China became a member of WTO on Dec. 11, 2001. Since then, nearly all TNCs worldwide prefer setting whole-owned subsidiary in China instead of a JV. Those who already married (those already have local partners and owns JV already) are pondering over, maneuvering to get ride of the existing local Chinese partners. JV Divorce cases are soaring, for example, P&G from USA, Danone from France.

Discussion:

1. Why do foreign companies prefer whole-owned subsidiary as a best entry mode into China since 2002?

2. What is the disadvantage of a JV?

3. Why do Chinese local partners lose value in the eyes of foreign partners?

4. Can you give some approaches and measures which the foreign partners take to get rid of Chinese partner? (for example, increase registered capital, control brand and downstream channels, etc.)

Online Practices:

1. Visit the Department of Commerce of PRC, click FDI Bureau（商务部外国投资管理司）www.fdi.gov.cn, consult more policy, info and data about FDI in China.

2. Visit the homepage of world No. 1 brewery - AB Inbev from Begium, www. ab-inbev. cn, learn the local brands which were M&A by AB-Inbv (for example, Haerbing Beer, Tsingtao Beer, Zhujiang Beer etc.).

3. Use internet to find more typical JV Divorce cases.

Case: Shanghai Auto M&A Ssangyong Motor Korea (2009) —4000 Million Loss

SAIC Motor Corporation Limited (informally SAIC, formerly Shanghai Automotive Industry Corporation) is a Chinese state-owned automotive manufacturing company headquartered in Shanghai, China with multinational operations. One of the "Big Four" Chinese automakers (along with Chang'an Motors, FAW Group, and Dongfeng Motor), the company had the largest production volume of any Chinese automaker in 2012 producing around 3. 5 million units. Its manufacturing mix likely includes a much smaller percentage of consumer offerings, as many SAIC passenger vehicles are pint-sized commercial vans.

At the start of the 2000s, SAIC made several acquisitions in Korea. In 2002 it participated in GM's purchase of Korean automaker Daewoo, acquiring a 10% stake in the newly formed GM Daewoo company for US $ 59. 7 million, and in 2004 it also assumed control of an ailing South Korean automaker, Ssangyong Motor, paying US $ 500 million for 48. 9% ownership of the company. Around this time SAIC created a new holding company for its subsidiaries employed in passenger car production, Shanghai Automotive Group.

Ssangyong Group is（双龙汽车）a South Korean based Chaebol or conglomerate. Ssangyong is best known for its sport-utility vehicles, sales of which have suffered recently due to the global economic downturn. Ssangyong, literally translated, means "Double Dragon". It was largely broken up by the East Asian financial crisis in 1997. The chaebol was forced to sell or relinquish control in many of their subsidiary interests including the Ssangyong Motor Company; the Ssangyong Paper Co., now controlled by Hankook P&G; Ssangyong Cement Industrial Co. Ltd., was owned by the shipping company, Afro-Asia; Yongpyung Resort, Ssangyong Heavy Industries, Ssangyong Precision Industry Co., Ssangyong Engineering & Construction Co. Ltd., and Riverside Cement, now controlled by Texas Industries, Inc; and Ssangyong Oil Refining Co., sold to Aramco in 1999.

On Jan. 9, 2009, Ssangyong Motor Co. filed for court receivership to avoid liquidation and seek time to return to profitability, as the Korean auto maker's top executives resigned. The move came after China's largest automotive firm, Shanghai Automotive Industry Corp., or SAIC — which owns a 51% stake in Ssangyong — gave up management rights over the troubled company. The company has been suffering from a serious liquidity crisis because of plummeting vehicle sales. The company had difficulties in raising funds due to a serious credit crunch globally. The receivership agreement will offer some protection from creditors and allows the auto maker to avoid formal bankruptcy. SAIC said that it will work with all parties so that Ssangyong can achieve a plan to normalize its operations. SAIC paid Ssangyong $ 45 million to provide short-term liquidity, but was reluctant to provide additional support, due to Ssangyong's high labor costs and slumping SUV demand. Korea Development Bank, Ssangyong's biggest creditor, threatened to take steps toward liquidation last year if SAIC pulled out.

Reference: Korean auto maker Ssangyong enters receivership. http://www.marketwatch.com/story/koreas-ssangyong-files-for-court-receivership? siteid=rss http://en.wikipedia.org/wiki/Shanghai_Automotive_Industry_Corporation;

http://en.wikipedia.org/wiki/Ssangyong

Discussion:

1. What reasons do you think which lead to the complete failure of the cross-border merger &acquisition?

2. SAIC at first initiated a labor layoff plan to reduce cost. But the labor force of Ssangyong occupied the factory and company as well as take up the weapons to fight with the "capitalist" from China. How do you look at such Labor-Capitalist conflicts?

Case: CFIUS - Foe of Chinese TNCs (2012)

The Committee on Foreign Investment in the United States (CFIUS, 美国外国投资委员会) has become a hot topic with the recent acquisition of Smithfield Foods by Chinese company Shuanghui International Holdings. The profile of CFIUS has been raised, but the actual process of how the committee reaches a verdict is still shrouded in mystery due to the confidentiality of the negotiations.

CFIUS is an entity of last resort that is a voluntary process but in practice, due to CFIUS's subpoena power, can easily become mandatory. The Committee is comprised of voting members (several government departments), non-voting members, and observers. The process consists of 30 days of review, 45 days of investigation, and 15 days allotted for presidential action. Common misconceptions about CFIUS include the notion that CFIUS changes rules on case-by-case basis, that CFIUS has been taken hostage by special interests, or that the committee is used for nationalistic or political reasons.

Huawei case：

"Little more than an exercise in China bashing." That is how a spokesman for Huawei has described a report published on October 8th by the Intelligence Committee of America's House of Representatives, which has spent the past year looking into the activities of two of China's biggest telecoms firms.

Among other things, the committee's report calls for any attempt by Huawei or ZTE to buy American companies to be blocked by a government body that is responsible for reviewing foreign purchases of American assets. It also says that the two firms' telecoms-networking equipment and components should be excluded from government systems and those of private firms that work on them.

If some of these recommendations are implemented, they could effectively stymie the Chinese firms' attempts to expand in the world's largest telecoms market and give a boost to rivals such as America's Cisco and Sweden's Ericsson.

The report itself fails to spell out any specific examples of the security risks that Huawei and ZTE pose. The Chinese firm also gave warning that shutting it out of the American market would create a "monstrous, trade-distorting precedent".

Indeed, knee-jerk techno-nationalism also makes no sense in an industry in which supply chains have become global. Most telecoms-equipment manufacturers now manufacture part or all of their kit in China and source components from the country. So what is needed most is an international effort to develop standards governing the integrity and security of telecoms networks. Sadly, the House Intelligence Committee isn't smart enough to see this.

Reference：M. G. | SAN FRANCISCO. http://www.economist.com/blogs/schumpeter/2012/10/chinese-telecoms-firms-america?sort=3#sort-comments 狙击华为

What Message is the US Sending on CFIUS? AmCham China News. http://www.amcham-china.org/article/11951 31 October 2013

Online Practices and Extended Reading：

1. Visit the website of CFIUS：www.ustreas.gov.

2. Use internet to find more typical cases which CFIUS blocked Chinese enterprises.（for example, Huawei exit USA forever（2013）；Sany Heavy Industrial case（2012）.

3. How do you think Chinese TNC can increase bargaining power with CFIUS?

Case：CHALCO M&A Rio Rinto：Failure and Lessons

China Aluminum Corp（CHALCO，中国铝业）initiated 19 Billion USA to M&A Rio Rinto.

Headquartered in UK, Rinto（力拓）was set up in 1873 and among the top 3 of global iron ore suppliers together with Vale and BHP. Due to global financial crisis, Rinto suffered huge losses and at that time eager to embrace the CHALCO. The transaction is about 19.5 billion USD, the huge amount M&A case was No. 1 cross-border M&A（merge and acquisition） initiated by a Chinese enterprises as well as No. 1 FDI inflow into Australia.

But from the beginning, there were great criticism and questioning from the Australian government and the public. Even Australian authorities and politicians such as the Premier Kevin Michael Rudd（陆克文）, but the Premier can speak fluent Mandarine/Chinese, always emphasis that the final decision is up to Rinto itself, but it was no-doubt that Australian authorities played critical role in the attitude change of Rinto.

Besides political reason, another economic reason also show strength. In May 2009, the international price for copper soared 70% to 5 145 USD/ ton, a historical summit. Rinto not only passed its most difficult time, but also saw huge profit windfall. For sure, no body will agree to sell a goose which lay gold eggs now.

On the side of China, some criticize that the long and exhausting domestic bureaucratic procedures which lag CHALCO behind of time, and thus give Rinto the breathing time to recovery.

The final is that Rinto gave CHALCO 19. 5 million USD as break-up fees and get rid of the Chinese guy. As a retaliation, on July 5, 2009, Chinese authorities and police arrested Hu Shitai（胡士泰）, the chief representatives of Rinto in Beijing, as commercial espionage.

Reference：

中铝收购力拓的政治色彩. http://www.ometal.com/bin/new/2009/6/8/china/20090608101148664754.htm

中铝投资力拓案的启示. http://finance.sina.com.cn/roll/20090619/10476372685.shtml

Extended Reading：Rio Tinto Espionage Case

The Rio Tinto espionage case began with the arrest on 5 July 2009, of four staff, headed by Hu Shitai（胡士泰）in the Shanghai office of the Rio Tinto Group, in the People's Republic of China, who were subsequently accused of bribery and espionage. Two days later, an import executive of the Shougang Group and Laigang Group was also arrested. The Rio Tinto employees, Australian Stern Hu and three Chinese colleagues, Wang Yong, Ge Minqiang and Liu Caikui, went on trial in Shanghai on Monday, 22 March 2010.

The government dropped the charges relating to the alleged theft of trade secrets before the trial, and the defendants admitted to having received bribes during the trial. Following the trial, Stern Hu was sentenced to 10 years jail. Hu and other convicted executives have also had their employment terminated by Rio Tinto Ltd. It is reported that the motive behind the terminations is in regards to a breach of conduct, with Rio Tinto accepting the evidence provided showing instances of bribery. Rio Tinto also states that the trial will not affect business ties, according to its chief executive. The arrests came during difficult negotiations over the price of iron ore for the 2009-2010 period.

Reference：http://en.wikipedia.org/wiki/Rio_Tinto_espionage_case

Discussion:

1. What lessons can we draw from the failure of Rinto M&A Case?

2. Hu Shitai is now spending his 10 years imprisonment in China jail now. It is said that Hu is just a scapegoat of Rinto. What is the high risks of being representatives of a foreign TNCs?

Online Practice:

Visit the website of ICSID (the World Bank's International Centre for Settlement of Investment Disputes) www. icsid.worldbank.org, learn its rules and application of international investment dispute settlement.

Case: FDI & OFDI of China (2013)

China is unique worldwide, because ODI and OFDI (outward FDI) of China both exceed 100 billion USD annually.

For a long time, China ranks No. 2 FDI inflow state worldwide, just after USA; while China ranks No. 1 FDI inflow among developing countries, with annual FDI inflow of 100 billion USD. At the same time, China ODI surged in 2012, and has now moved into the "fast lane" internationally, ranking No. 5 worldwide.

For example, Chinese investment in Russia jumped 117. 8 percent year-on-year in 2012, while investment in the United States increased 66. 4 percent year-on-year and it was up 47. 8 percent year-on-year in Japan. Chinese non-financial ODI in ASEAN countries rose 52 percent year-on-year in 2012. China's provincial investors' ODI was $ 28. 19 billion or 36. 5 percent of China's total non-financial ODI in 2012, up 38. 9 percent year-on-year. The provinces of Guangdong, Shandong, Jiangsu, Liaoning and Zhejiang are top investors in overseas destinations.

As domestic enterprises continue to use global resources, and seek more opportunities in overseas markets, that momentum will continue into the future, as long as supportive policies are not changed. China's ODI has moved into the fast lane.

Statistics released by the Ministry of Commerce, the National Bureau of Statistics and the State Administration of Foreign Exchange showed that non-financial FDI stock already exceed 1 trillion USD in July 2012, while the OFDI stock about 443 billion USD.

CHINA'S NON-FINANCIAL OUTBOUND DIRECT INVESTMENT

Unit: $ billion

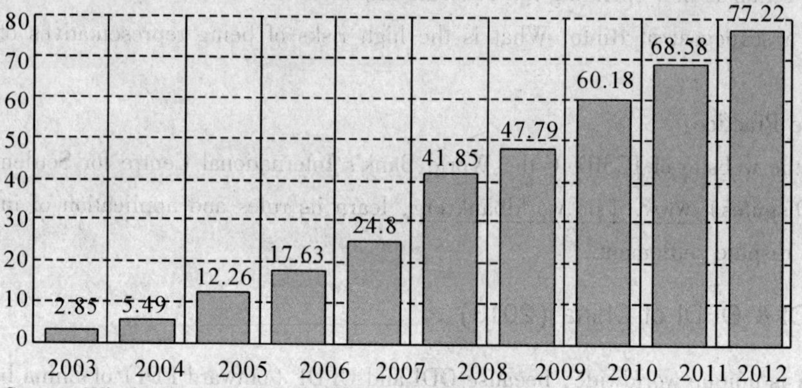

Source: Wind Information

CHINA DAILY

Reference: Li Jiabao, China's non-financial ODI enters "fast lane". http://www.chinadaily.com.cn/business/2013-01/17/content_16130679.htm;

CHAPTER 8
Regional Economic Integration

At the end of this chapter, you should be able to:

- Understand the different level of regional integration;
- Explain the boom of REs worldwide;
- Understand the economic and political argument of REs;
- Be familiar with the Res which china is involved and their impacts.

Case: Shanghai FTZ (2013)

In August 2013, the State Council of PRC approved the establishment of a pilot free trade zone (FTZ) in Shanghai, moving it closer to becoming a global financial, trade and shipping hub to rival other Asian cities such as Hong Kong. China already has two free trade zones, one in Hong Kong and one in Shenzhen. China aims to lift the zone up to international standards featuring convenient investment and trade, free exchange of currencies, efficient supervision and a sound legal environment after two to three years of test operation. An FTZ could attract investors only when it has advantages in tariff policy, logistics cost and clearance efficiency, which will be decided by its operator's capability in institutional innovation and management. The free trade zone is a integrated concept, which includes the opening of finance, trade, investment and administration. Chinese policymakers are clear about foreign investors' concerns and are trying to find a solution through the construction and improvement of the FTZ.

Reference:

Shanghai FTZ to create favorable "micro-environment" for investment. http://news.xinhuanet.com/english/china/2013-09/29/c_132762303.htm

Extended Reading: China-ASEAN FTA (2010)

The China-ASEAN Free Trade Area, also known as ASEAN-China Free Trade Area (ACFTA) is a free trade area among the ten member states of the Association of Southeast Asian Nations (ASEAN) and the People's Republic of China. The member states of ASEAN include Singapore, Brunei, Laos, Malaysia, Vietnam, Cambodia, Burma, Philippines, Indonesia, Thailand.

The initial framework agreement was signed on 4 November 2002 in Phnom Penh, Cambodia, with the intent on establishing a free trade area among the eleven nations by 2010. The free trade area came into effect on 1 January 2010. The ASEAN-China Free Trade Area is the largest free trade area in terms of population and third largest in terms of nominal GDP.

Since the launch out of China-ASEAN FTA, mutual trade and investment are in boom. In 2011, ASEAN took the place ofJapan and became No. 3 trade partner of China. In 2013, trade volume between China and ASEAN was 443.6 Billion USD.

Reference: http://en.wikipedia.org/wiki/ASEAN%E2%80%93China_Free_Trade_Area;

东盟取代日本成中国第三大贸易伙伴 http://www.caexpo.com/news/special/economy/2011dmqdrb/.

Online Practices:

Visit: www.asean-cn.org, learn more policies, info, trend of China-Asean.

Extended Reading: CEPA (2003)

CEPA(Closer Economic Partnership Arrangement)《关于建立更紧密经贸关系的安排》

The Mainland and Macau Closer Economic Partnership Arrangement, or Closer Economic Partnership Arrangement (CEPA) for short, is an economic agreement between the Government of the Macau Special Administrative Region and the Central People's Government on October 18, 2003. A similar agreement, known as the Mainland and Hong Kong Closer Economic Partnership Arrangement, was signed between the Government of the Hong Kong Special Administrative Region and the Central People's Government of the People's Republic of China, signed on June 29, 2003.

Regular supplements with further liberalisations have been signed between the Mainland and Macau governments. The most recent, Supplement VIII (also referred to as CEPA VIII), was signed in December 2011 and enters into effect on 1 April 2012.

CEPA is stated to have the following objectives: "To strengthen trade and investment cooperation between Mainland China and Macau and promote joint development of the two sides, through the implementation of the following measures: 1. progressively reducing or eliminating tariffs and non-tariff barriers on substantially all the trade in goods between the two sides; 2. progressively achieving liberalization of trade in services through reduction or elimination of substantially all discriminatory measures; 3. promoting trade and investment facilitation."

The Annexes to CEPA elaborate measures to achieve these objectives and detail how products and service providers can qualify for the CEPA benefits, including: 1. Arrangement for Implementation of Zero Tariff for Trade in Goods (Annex 1); 2. Rules of Origin for Trade in Goods (Annex 2); 3. Procedures for the Issuing and Verification of Certificates of Origin (Annex 3); 4. Specific Commitments on Liberalization of Trade in Services (Annex 4); 5. Definition of "Service Supplier" and Related Requirements (Annex 5); 6. Trade and Investment Facilitation (Annex 6).

Reference: http://en.wikipedia.org/wiki/Mainland_and_Macau_Closer_Economic_Partnership_Arrangement

Discussion:

1. WTO is a global comprehensiveframework for international trade and investment. But its is most strange that sovereignty states worldwide are enthusiastic about setting up regional integration (RI). In 1960s, there were 19 RI, now more than 200. Could you think about some reasons for RI fans?

2. Please discuss world most advanced and most successful regional integration: EU.

3. Please use the internet to search as more aspossible the regional integration organization which China participated or initiated, for example APEC...

4. In 2013, President Obama was absent from APEC Summit, please discuss the dilemma of APEC.

Extended Reading:

TPP (Trans -Pacific Partnership Agreement, 跨太平洋伙伴关系)

The embryo of TPP is Trans-Pacific Strategic Economic Partnership Agreement, P4. P4 was initiated by New Zealand, Singapore, Chile and Brunei with the aim to accelerate the trade liberalization of Asia-Pacific regions. On Nov. 11, 2011, Japan joined TPP. On Sep. 10, South Korea jointed TPP. TPP model is a comprehensive package, including all goods and services with the aim of launching officially at the end of 2013.

TTIP (Transatlantic Trade and Investment Partnership, 跨大西洋贸易与投资伙伴协定)

The Transatlantic Trade and Investment Partnership (TTIP) also known as the Transatlantic Free Trade Area (TAFTA) is a proposed free trade agreement between the European Union and the United States. Proponents say the agreement would result in multilateral economic growth, while critics say it would increase corporate power and make it more difficult for governments to regulate markets for public benefit. The U. S. government considers the TTIP a companion agreement to the Trans-Pacific Partnership. After a proposed draft was leaked, in March 2014 the European Commission launched a public consultation on a limited set of clauses. A previous proposed treaty was Multilateral Agreement on Investment. The TTIP free trade agreement could be finalised by the end of 2014.

TTIP covers:

Market Access : Removing custom duties on goods and restrictions on services, gaining better access to public markets, and making it easier to invest. Industry-specific regulation.

Industry - specific regulation: Improved regulatory coherence and cooperation by dismantling unnecessary regulatory barriers such as bureaucratic duplication of effort Broader rules and principles and modes of co-operation.

Broader rules and principles and modes of co-operation : Improved cooperation when it comes to setting international standards.

Reference: http://en.wikipedia.org/wiki/Transatlantic_Trade_and_Investment_Partnership

Discussion:

1. Taking great efforts, in 2001 China joined WTO, the global multi-lateral trade and investment framework. But it seems WTO will be replaced by new world arena: TPP and TTIP. How do you look at such world trade arena and investment framework?

2. It is said that TPP and TTIP are set up especially aiming at restrainting China. How do you think of this view point?

PART FOUR
The Global Monetary System

CHAPTER 9
The Foreign Exchange Market

At the end of this chapter, you should be able to:

· Understand the functions and unique features of foreign exchange market;

· Understand the basic theories of rate determination AND FORCASTING;

· Be familiar with basic FX operations, such as SHORT;

· Understand EX Risk reduction approaches, such as the hedgestrategy.

Case: Samsung Hedging Strategy Technical Analyst (2012)

A hedge is an investment position intended to offset potential losses/gains that may be incurred by a companion investment. In simple language, a hedge is used to reduce any substantial losses/gains suffered by an individual or an organization. A hedge can be constructed from many types of financial instruments, including stocks, exchange-traded funds, insurance, forward contracts, swaps, options, many types of over-the-counter and derivative products, and future contracts. Public futures markets were established in the 19th century to allow transparent, standardized, and efficient hedging of agricultural commodity prices; they have since expanded to include futures contracts for hedging the values of energy, precious metals, foreign currency, and interest rate fluctuations.

Samsung Hedging Strategy: Time-adjusted P/E-based oversold strategy.

Our time-adjusted P/E-based oversold strategy is a contrarian approach that focuses on oversold stocks based on time-adjusted P/E multiples and absolute share prices. The long portfolio consists of 15 equally-weighted stocks chosen from the top-100 Kospi stocks by market cap.

January 31, 2012

Beginning Feb 1, we add to our portfolio auto stocks such as Hyundai Mobis, Mando, Hyundai Motor, and Hankook Tire, which plunged recently after the announcement of sluggish 4Q earnings—we consider them oversold. Also now included are industrials stocks. Relative-strength-based trading strategy For the week ending Jan 31, our strong-momentum portfolio gained 1.5%, while the weak momentum portfolio lost 4%—the Kospi gained 3.33% during the week. Looking ahead to the week beginning Feb 1, LG Uplus, Cheil Worldwide, and NHN look to have the strongest momentum, while OCI, Hanwha Chemical, and GS appear to have the least. Over Jan 18-Jan 31, we opened the following trading pairs: long Huchems Fine

Chemical/short Capro, long Mando/short Halla Climate Control, long Shinsegae/short Lotte Shopping, long Mando/short Hankook Tire, long Dongyang Mechatronics/short Kumho Tire, long KT/short SK Telecom, long Foosung/short Huchems Fine Chemical, and long Tong Yang Life/short Meritz Fire & Marine. Weekly fund flow Despite substantial net buying by foreign investors, the Kospi gained just 0. 8% over Jan 25-27 as domestic institutional investors net sold considerably. Domestic institutional investors preferred stocks in the energy, electronics, food & beverage, and display sectors, but sold in the autos, shipbuilding, semiconductors, and chemical sectors. Foreign investors bought in the semiconductors, chemicals, banking, and steel sectors while selling in the food & beverage and telecom sectors.

Feb 1, 2012

we add to our portfolio auto stocks such as Hyundai Mobis, Mando, Hyundai Motor, and Hankook Tire, which plunged recently after the announcement of sluggish 4Q earnings—we consider them oversold. Also now included are industrials stocks. Consumer Discretionary Mando Consumer Discretionary Hyundai Glovis Industrials Hyundai Motor Consumer Discretionary Hankook Tire Consumer Discretionary LG Household & Consumer Health Care Staples S1 Industrials Consumer Staples Materials.

Reference: Dong Young Kim. http://bg.panlv.net/report/2170f294eda3515f.html http://en.wikipedia.org/wiki/Hedge_(finance)

Case: Soros Attack JPY (2013), HKD (2007) & GBP (1992)

In July 2013, a hedge fund run by billionaire investor George Soros was back placing bets in Japan, shorting the yen and snapping up local stocksr. Soros returned to the market following some signs of stability in the Japanese bond market. While the sharp recent fall in Japanese equities was a "surprise", the current level of stocks was "very attractive" as economic data and earnings were expected to pick up. The Nikkei Stock Average /quotes/zigman/5986735/delayed JP: NIK +0. 62% fell 2. 1% in Friday's afternoon trading, and had entered a so-called bear market after dropping more than 20% from its 52-week peak reached on May 23. The U. S. dollar /quotes/zigman/4868099/realtime/sampled USDJPY -0. 0187%, meanwhile, was trading at ¥96. 34, also sharply down from its May highs above ¥103.

In 2007, currency speculators aim to force an end to pegging arrangement with US dollar: Soros challenges Chinese over Hong Kong dollar. Soros amassed sources quickly speculate and attacks on HKD. For as long as those holding Hong Kong dollar assets remain confident in the currency, there is very little that speculators without Hong Kong dollar assets can do in the market to destabilize our currency and make a profit. Soros have to borrow in order to cover their short Hong Kong dollar positions, and as the lender of last resort for Hong Kong dollars, the Hong Kong Monetary Authority (HKMA) will not lend cheaply, directly or indirectly, to speculators. Financial institutions serving as lenders of first resort to borrowers will also not fund speculators cheaply and expose themselves to the risks of a funding squeeze. Confidence in our stable currency was unaffected. The exchange rate hardly moved.

In 1997, In the week leading up to September 16, 1992 or "Black Wednesday", Quantum Funds earned $ 1.8 billion by shorting British pounds and buying German marks. This transaction earned Soros the title of "the Man Who Broke the Bank of England" and force UK exit from ERM. On the other hand, British government policy in the period before the ejection of the pound sterling from the Exchange Rate Mechanism of the European Monetary System had been widely criticised for providing speculators with a one-way bet.

What is ERM?

The European Exchange Rate Mechanism (ERM) was a system introduced by the European Community in March 1979, as part of the European Monetary System (EMS), to reduce exchange rate variability and achieve monetary stability in Europe, in preparation for Economic and Monetary Union and the introduction of a single currency, the euro, which took place on 1 January 1999.

The ERM is based on the concept of fixed currency exchange rate margins, but with exchange rates variable within those margins. This is also known as a semi-pegged system. Before the introduction of the euro, exchange rates were based on the European Currency Unit (ECU), the European unit of account, whose value was determined as a weighted average of the participating currencies. A grid (known as the Parity Grid) of bilateral rates was calculated on the basis of these central rates expressed in ECUs, and currency fluctuations had to be contained within a margin of 2.25% on either side of the bilateral rates (with the exception of the Italian lira, the Spanish peseta, the Portuguese escudo and the pound sterling, which were allowed to fluctuate by ±6%). Determined intervention and loan arrangements protected the participating currencies from greater exchange rate fluctuations.

After the adoption of the euro, policy changed to linking currencies of countries outside the eurozone to the euro (having the common currency as a central point). The goal was to improve stability of those currencies, as well as to gain an evaluation mechanism for potential eurozone members. This mechanism is known as ERM II and has superseded ERM. Currently there are just two countries in the ERM II, the Danish krone and the Lithuanian litas.

Reference: Soros shorting yen, buying Japan stock http://www.marketwatch.com/story/soros-shorting-yen-buying-japan-stocks-report-2013-06-06

http://en.wikipedia.org/wiki/Soros_Fund_Management; http://www.rense.com/general90/euro.htm hkma.gov.hk/eng/key - information/speech - speakers/jckyam/speech_180996b.shtml

http://en.wikipedia.org/wiki/European_Exchange_Rate_Mechanism

Discussion:

1. How to use SHORT position（卖空操作）to attack a fixed exchange rate states?

2. Why do we say such attack is a one-way bet? That is the international speculators can estimate and know in advance the exact timing and maximum cost of such success?

3. Please compare the attack tactics for different cases, please focus on evolution and innovation of attack skills!

4. Why does UK prefer to be out of Euro zone?

Extended Reading: Linked Exchange Rate System in Hong Kong

Linked exchange rate is in fact a kind of currency board system. A currency board is a monetary authority which is required to maintain a fixed exchange rate with a foreign currency. This policy objective requires the conventional objectives of a central bank to be subordinated to the exchange rate target. The main qualities of an orthodox currency board are:

· A currency board's foreign currency reserves must be sufficient to ensure that all holders of its notes and coins (and all banks creditor of a Reserve Account at the currency board) can convert them into the reserve currency (usually 110%~115% of the monetary base M0).

· A currency board maintains absolute, unlimited convertibility between its notes and coins and the currency against which they are pegged (the anchor currency), at a fixed rate of exchange, with no restrictions on current-account or capital-account transactions.

· A currency board only earns profit from interests on foreign reserves (less the expense of note-issuing), and does not engage in forward-exchange transactions. These foreign reserves exist (1) because local notes have been issued in exchange, or (2) because commercial banks must by regulation deposit a minimum reserve at the Currency Board. (1) generates a seignorage revenue. (2) is the revenue on minimum reserves (revenue of investment activities less cost of minimum reserves remuneration)

· A currency board has no discretionary powers to affect monetary policy and does not lend to the government. Governments cannot print money, and can only tax or borrow to meet their spending commitments.

· A currency board does not act as a lender of last resort to commercial banks, and does not regulate reserve requirements.

· A currency board does not attempt to manipulate interest rates by establishing a discount rate like a central bank. The peg with the foreign currency tends to keep interest rates and inflation very closely aligned to those in the country against whose currency the peg is fixed.

Hong Kong operates a currency board (Hong Kong Monetary Authority), as do Bulgaria and Lithuania. Estonia had a currency board fixed to the Deutsche Mark from 1992 to 1999 when it switched to fixing to the Euro at par. The peg to the Euro was upheld until January 2011 with Estonia's adoption of the Euro. This policy is seen as a mainstay of that country's subsequent economic success (see Economy of Estonia for a detailed description of the Estonian currency board). Argentina abandoned its currency board in January 2002 after a severe recession. The British Overseas Territories of Gibraltar, the Falkland Islands and St. Helena continue to operate currency boards, backing their locally printed currency notes with pound sterling reserves.

Reference: http://en.wikipedia.org/wiki/Currency_board

Discussion:

Currency board (发钞局制度) is an extremely strict fixed exchange rate system and are ready to suffer speculative attack. Why did Hong Kong etc. choose this system (联系汇率制度)?

Online Documentary and Reading:

1. http://video.sina.com.cn/v/b/28043981-1605259015.html 英镑狙击战

2. http://video.sina.com.cn/v/b/28043981-1605259015.html#11797514 揭秘金融大鳄

3. http://www.tudou.com/programs/view/-8JwCgHOqTs/ 央视采访 Soros

4. Visit the website of Morgan Stanley www.morganstanleychain.com, learn the financial terminology systematically.

CHAPTER 10
The International Monetary System

At the end of this chapter, you should be able to:

· Understand the evolution of international monetary system;

· Underseand the role IMF and World Bank & world financial crisis;

· Underseand fixed & floating exchange rate system;

· Underseand the existing international reserves system and its pro and cons;

· Underseand Currency Board & Linked Exchange Rate.

Case: IMF Does More Harm than Good? (2014)

The European Commission has expressed "fundamental disagreement" with a "plainly wrong" IMF report that has accused the EU of sacrificing Greece to save the euro from debt crisis contagion.

The Brussels executive has responded with barely contained fury to a Fund report, drawn up by its staff in Washington, which identified "notable failures" in the EU-IMF bailouts of Greece, beginning in 2010. The IMF's criticism centered on claims that the EU was more concerned with propping up the euro than saving Greece and failed to identify growth friendly reforms for the highly indebted southern European country.

With hindsight we can go back and say in an ideal world what should have been done differently. The circumstances were what they were. I think the commission did its best in an unprecedented situation. The accusation of hindsight bias was repeated by Mario Draghi, head of the European Central Bank, which, while escaping direct IMF criticism, led the EU's refusal to consider writing down Greek debt for two years.

By 2006, IMF was committing loans to more than 60 countries that were struggling with economic and currency crises. All IMF loan packages came with various conditions attached. In general, IMF will insist on a combination of tight economic macroeconomic policy, including cuts in public spending, higher interest rate and tight monetary policy. IMF often pushed fro deregulation of sectors formerly protected ted from domestic and foreign competition, large scale privatization of SOEs etc.

Many recipient states complained that IMF package is am inappropriate polices and they are all "one therapy for all", that is on matter which country, what kind of crisis, IMF always give one-size-fit-all solution. For example, during Asian Crisis, South Korean took IMF loans and follow the therapy by IMF, the result was more than 100 financial institutions went bankrupt and 1/10 workforce nationwide lost job.

If further investigating IMF in details, USA is No. 1 Quota owner, about 16.75% share and corresponding voting rights. No. 2 is China with small share with 3.807%. According to the rule of IMF, the passing of decision in IMF should have more than 85% voting rights (supermajority). Simple calculation will tell us a truth: in IMF, without the support of USA, there will be no decisions can be passed.

Reference: Brussels dismisses "plainly wrong" IMF criticism over Greece http://www.telegraph.co.uk/finance/financialcrisis/10103912/Brussels-dismisses-plainly-wrong-IMF-criticism-over-Greece.html

Extension Case: BRICs Set Up Their Own IMF? (2014)

BRICS is the acronym for an association of five majoremerging national economies: Brazil, Russia, India, China, and South Africa. The grouping was originally known as "BRIC" before the inclusion of South Africa in 2010. The BRICS members are all developing or newly industrialised countries, but they are distinguished by their large, fast-growing economies and significant influence on regional and global affairs; all five are G-20 members. As of 2014, the five BRICS countries represent almost 3 billion people which is 40% of the world population, with a combined nominal GDP of US $ 16.039 trillion (20% world GDP) and an estimated US $ 4 trillion in combined foreign reserves. As of 2014, the BRICS nations represented 18 percent of the world economy.

Considering the limited and questionable role of IMF as well as China's 4 Trillion USD international reserves, BRICS next year will set up its own IMF and the World Bank. In 2012, BRICS countries to push for more influence at the IMF, they currently only hold about a combined 11% of the Fund's voting shares. By way of comparison, the U. S. holds a 16.75% voting share, allowing it to veto any major decision, which require an 85% supermajority, while the United Kingdom and France both have larger voting shares than any of the BRIC countries singularly.

In setting up the development bank, the BRICS would be mounting a challenge to global institutions like the World Bank and the European Bank for Reconstruction and Development, which attach political conditions to the low-interest loans they disburse to developing countries. In contrast, the BRICS development bank is expected to offer non-conditional loans at a higher interest rate. At the same time, it has been suggested that the BRICS bank could augment the World Bank by funding projects in industries that the World Bank does not, such as biofuels, large dams and nuclear power plants, which don't meet the World Bank's environmental standards. The proposed bailout mechanism, on the other hand, could act as an alternative to global financial institutions like the International Monetary Fund. If so, the bailout fund could also significantly enhance the BRICS countries international stature and influence. At the same time, this bloc is reportedly considering linking the bailout fund partially or in whole to the IMF or another Bretton Woods institution, much as ASEAN+3 decided to do in establishing the Chiang Mai Initiative, a similar pooled fund designed to inject liquidity into markets and minimize the impact of external shocks.

On July 10, 2014, BRICS announced to already set up their own development bank with initial capital of 100 billion USD. It is estimated in 2014, BRICS will contribute 61.3% of global economic growth.

Reference: BRICS set up their own IMF. http://rbth.com/business/2014/04/14/brics_countries_to_set_up_their_own_imf_35891.html

BRICS: The WorldNew Banker. http://thediplomat.com/2012/11/brics-the-worlds-new-banker/

Discussion:

1. The pros and cons of IMF and its regional counter-partner, for example, BRICS, Development Bank.

2. Please search the internet to find the reactions from USA and EU.

Case: New Reserve Currency to Challenge the Dollar (2011)

The IMF is trying to move the world away from the U. S. dollar and towards a global currency once again. Inits report entitled "Enhancing International Monetary Stability—A Role for the SDR", the IMF details the "problems" with having the U. S. dollar as the reserve currency of the globe and the IMF discusses the potential for a larger role for SDRs (Special Drawing Rights). But the IMF certainly does not view SDRs as the "final solution" to global currency problems. Rather, the IMF considers SDRs to be a transitional phase between what we have now and a new world currency. IMF makes this point very clearly: "In the even longer run, if there were political willingness to do so, these securities could constitute an embryo of global currency."

The SDR is supposed to be "an embryo" from which a global currency will one day develop. The SDR is a hybrid. SDRs are part U. S. dollar, part euro, part yen and part British pound. In particular, the following is how each SDR currently breaks down: U. S. Dollar: 41.9%; Euro: 37.4%; Yen: 9.4%; British Pound: 11.3%. But there calls for other national currencies to be included in the basket. Russian President Dmitry Medvedev has publicly called for the national currencies of Brazil, Russia, India and China to be included in the SDR. The Obama administration said that it fully supports the eventual inclusion of the yuan in the SDR.

"A global currency, bancor, issued by a global central bank would be designed as a stable store of value that is not tied exclusively to the conditions of any particular economy. As trade and finance continue to grow rapidly and global integration increases, the importance of this broader perspective is expected to continue growing."

Reference: Michael Snyder. The U. S. Dollar Needs To Be Replaced As The World Reserve Currency And SDRs "Could Constitute An Embryo Of Global Currency". http://the economic collapseblog.com/archives/shocking-new-imf-report-the-u-s-dollar-needs-to-be-replaced-as-the-world-reserve-currency-and-that-sdrs-could-constitute-an-embryo-of-global-currencyFebruary 11th, 2011

Discussion:

1. What is the problems of USD as the world main reserve currency? What is "Triffin Dilemma" (confidence & liquidity of a reserve currency)?

2. President Obama answered Mr. Zhou Xiaochuan, the governor of the People's Bank of China, "there is no need to create a new world currency taking the place of USD." How do you look at the world currency debate across countries?

Case: RMB to Be Third Largest International Currency by 2020 (2014)

The Chinese currency yuan will become the world's third largest currency after the US dollar and Euro by 2020. A report by the International Monetary Institute of Renmin University of China and the Bank of Communications, published on Sunday, said that the Yuan internationalization index had risen to 1.69 by the end of 2013 from 0.92 a year before. The main impetuses for the internationalization of the yuan come from cross-border trade settlement and direct investment. In 2013, China's cross-border yuan trade settlement hit 4.63 trillion yuan ($759 billion), up 57.5 percent year on year, and Yuan direct investment totaled 534 billion yuan, up 90 percent year on year. The institute and the bank have been jointly issuing Yuan internationalization reports annually since 2012.

The Chinese government launched RMB settlement for transnational trade in 2009, the beginnings of an attempt to push RMB into the international settlement system. The effect, though, will depend on whichever the settlement system is accepted by trading partners.

Five departments, including the central bank and the Ministry of Finance, released rules and set principles for RMB settlement in transnational trade. Shanghai will become the first pilot city for the operation of RMB settlement, followed by Guangdong Province. The Bank of

China and Bank of Communications are the first banks to be approved to operate such settlement.

In 2009, China's foreign trade is mainly settled by USD and the Euro. The Chinese government is promoting RMB to be the settlement currency in Asia. This may first come to pass in Hong Kong. Hong Kong has long sought to reinforce its ties with the mainland, and in the future HKD will likely be pegged to RMB rather than the dollar. Chinese importers and exporters will certainly welcome a RMB settlement system, as it will help them avoid exchange rate risk. The problem will come in the preferences of overseas traders.

Reference：http://www.chinastakes.com/2009/7/rmb-ready-to-become-international-settlement-currency.html

http://www.chinadaily.com.cn/business/2014-07/21/content_17874392. htm

Discussion：

How did a sovereignty currency evolve from a domestic currency to an international settlement currency, then international investment currency and finally the international reserve currency?

Online Lectures by Top University：

The Role of the Renminbi in the International Monetary System. (The Chinese University of Hong Kong, http://mooc.guokr.com/course/251/The-Role-of-the-Renminbi-in-the-International-Monetary-System/)

Case：$ 4 Trillion International Reserves Dilemma (2014)

China's foreign exchange reserves rose by a faster-than-expected 30. 3 percent year-on-year by 2014 to reach $ 4 trillion. The country increased its holdings of US Treasury bonds, the US debt holdings, according to the US Treasury Department.

Although many adviser to the People's Bank of China has repeatedly called on the government to reduce the holdings of US Treasury bonds and to halt future purchases as the dollar will probably continue to weaken. But some analysts said that a massive sell-off of US bonds would be financial suicide for China as it would drive down the value of its own holdings. They added that Beijing is faced with a dilemma as it has little option but to keep buying US bonds to calm jittery markets.

Just as Chinese officials have pledged to continue buying euro zone debt at various points, China is likely to react by emphasizing that the central bank will continue to buy Treasuries. Both China and the US are interlinked in a search for prosperity and to keep both economies afloat.

Reference：Li Xiang and Li Xing. China's foreign reserves dilemma. http://www.chinadaily.com.cn/china/2011-08/02/content_13028341. htm

Discussion：

1. How was the $ 4 trillion reserves accumulated during a short time?

2. China experienced high liquidity domestic, or more simply high inflation at home. How domestic liquidity is interlinked with world reserves currency? What is Seigniorage (储备货币国家铸币税) and " Inflation Tax"?

3. Besides continuous purchasing US treasury bond/bill, could you propose more outlet for our huge reserves?

Case: Chinese Grandma: Gold Rollercoaster (2013-2014)

The story of Chinese grandma (dama) fall into two part. The first part happed in 2013, when the freefall of gold price stirs Chinese dama's spending spree on gold in and dama feel that they win the Wall Street totally. While in 2014, the whole world see Chinese Dama completely hung up by gold due to the sharp decrease of gold price.

The freefall of gold price stirs Chinese consumers' spending spree on gold in 2013. The bargain-hunting middle-aged Chinese women known as "dama", have exerted the influence of the rising Chinese middle class in the gold market. Throughout 2013, the global gold market has risen and fallen in line with expectations that the Federal Reserve would withdraw its quantitative easing (QE) stimulus. Gold has fallen 29 percent in 2013, and is heading for the biggest annual loss in 32 years. Gold prices took off from $ 800 an ounce after the Fed started the first round of QE, known as QE1, in 2008, and then QE2 propped up the price to an all-time high of $ 1 920 an ounce in September of 2011. Worries about inflation in the US continued to impel investor demand for gold. Although the price fell to around $ 1 600, two months later it was soon pushed up to $ 1 800 by QE3. Gold lost $ 200 an ounce in two trading days in April this year, a result of the recovering US economy and growing calls for scaling back QE. However, Chinese consumers are not deterred by the falling prices that have continued throughout this year. May 2013, **Dama bought 300 tons gold in 10 days, which is about 10% of world gold output.**

But in Jan. 2014, the price of gold fell to 725 USD/ ton, the Chinese dama are completely hung up.

Reference: Did Chinese dama lose big on gold? http://news.xinhuanet.com/english/china/2014-01/01/c_133011585.htm

Discussion:

1. What's the evolution of world gold reserves? Why is the price of gold volatile recently? Why were Chinese grandmas hung up?

2. The following chart specifies the gold reserves in various states. It is shocking to see the Europeans countries own gold reserves more than 70%~90%, but China is only 1.6%. How do you look at this phenomenon?

Ranking	States	Official Gold Reserves (ton)	Gold Reserves/Total Foreign Reserves (%)
1	USA	8 133.50	75.1
2	Germany	3 395.50	71.9
3	IMF	2 814.00	/
4	Italy	2 451.80	71.3
5	France	2 435.40	71.6
6	China	1 054.10	1.6
7	Switzerland	1 040.10	14.2
8	Russia	918	9.2
9	Japan	765.2	3.1
10	Netherland	612.5	60.2
11	India	557.7	9.8
12	ECB	502.1	32
13	Taiwan, China	422.7	5.6
14	Portugal	382.5	89.9
15	Venezuela	365.8	74.8

Online Practices and Extended Reading:

1. Visit the website of World Gold Council（WGC，世界黄金协会）www.gold.org, please consult the up-to-date ranking of gold reserves.

2. Watch onlinedocumentary: Fort Knox Gold Pool（美国诺克斯堡黄金库）http://www.verycd.com/topics/218968/.

3. Gold Pool of New York Reserve Bank（纽约储备银行外国银行黄金库）http://news.sohu.com/20080920/n259654229.shtml.

CHAPTER 11
The Global Capital Market

At the end of this chapter, you should be able to:

· Understand the framework of global capital markets;

· Be familiar with different longterm capital instruments, such as stock and bond;

· Know detailed on-field operations and tactics to raise capital;

· Understand the difference of world main stock exchanges;

· Know the huge risks incurred by improper capital-raising.

Case: China's Banking Pick Up Strategic Investors (2005&2011) -lessons and costs paid

China Banking Regulatory Commission (CBRC) was authorized by law to regulate and supervise all the banking institutions in China and their business activities. By October 2005, China's banking system consisted of more than 30 000 institutions, including 3 policy banks, 4 state-owned commercial banks (SOCBs), 13 joint-stock commercial banks (JSCBs, including the newly-established China Bohai Bank Co., Ltd), 115 city commercial banks, 626 urban credit cooperatives (UCCs), 30, 438 rural credit cooperatives, 57 rural cooperative/commercial banks, 238 operational entities of foreign banks, 4 asset management companies (AMCs), 59 trust and investment companies (TICs), 74 finance companies affiliated to business groups, 12 financial leasing companies, 5 auto financing companies, plus a large number of postal savings institutions scattered around the country.

The CBRC has pushed ahead the so-called reform of Chinese banking institutions and made new remarkable achievements., including urging and require all the state-owned commercial banks to attract foreign strategic investors.

In a follow-up to the launch of pilot joint-stock restructuring of BOC and CCB in 2003, ICBC was approved by the State Council i to start its joint-stock reform. So far, the four large reforming banks, namely BOC, CCB, ICBC and BOC have oversea strategic investors abroad. For example, BOA (Bank of America) took 19.9% equity of CCB with a price only 0.1428 USD per share (initially paid 2.5 billion USD to buy 17.5 billion shares). Similar story happed to other overseas strategic investors, for example, Temasek, the state sovereignty wealth fund from Singapore, paid only 1.466 billion USD and took 5.1% equity of CCB, the price is 0.94 HKD per share only! In 2006, Goldman Sachs tighter with Allianz paid only

3. 78 billion USD and took 10% equity of ICBC with a price of 1. 16 per share. All the overseas profited tremendously from their Chinese partners, for example, immediately after the listing of CCB In Hong Kong, its share price jumped immediately 156%. By 2011, during the six years which BOA as the strategic investors of CCB, BOA encashed its partial shares of CCB and gained 7. 5 billion USD profit. April 2014, Goldman Sachs and Och-Ziff are among the companies preparing final bids for part of a strategic stake in China's banks.

Reference: Latest Developments in China's Banking Reform, Opening - up and Supervision. China Banking Regulatory Commission (December 5, 2005). http://money.163. com/05/1205/13/247C68G100251GNK.html;

Discussion:

1. Why did China's banks, for example CCB and ICBC etc., become the cash cow of their overseas strategic investors?

2. Why did China Banking Regulatory Commission (CBRC) abandon the regulations that the Chinese banks must have an overseas strategic investors on Dec. 28, 2006?

3. ABC, Agricultural Bank of China, is the last one to be listed in A and H share. ABC, as the smartest one, learned the lessons of CCB and ICBC and didn't have a foreign strategic investors. How do you look at this phenomenon?

4. Please discuss with your partners the approach and ways used by foreign strategic investors to take control of China's banks.

Online Practices:

1. Use internet to find as many as you can all the overseas strategic investors of China's banks. Please learn their equity proportion and the price, as well as the profit they gained during these years.

2. Visit the website of China's sovereignty wealth fund company, China Investment Company www.china-inv.cn. Please compare China Investment Company with Temasek, the sovereignty wealth fund company from Singapore.

Case: Alibaba Listing—The Largest IPO in USA (2014)

Chinese e-commerce giant Alibaba Group Holding officially filed. In May, 2014 to go public in the US in what could be the largest initial public offering ever. A regulatory filing gave a $ 1 billion place holder value for the offering, but the actual amount is expected to be far higher, possibly exceeding $ 20 billion and topping not only Facebook's $ 16 billion 2012 listing, but Agricultural Bank of China Ltd. 's record $ 22. 1 billion offering in Shanghai and Hong Kong in 2010.

Alibaba, founded by former English teacher Jack Ma in a Hangzhou apartment, and its bankers have been moving to throw their own shares behind the IPO, analysts have said. In its filing Alibaba gave no date for the proposed IPO or whether it would be on the New York Stock Exchange or Nasdaq; the two exchange are fighting to win the Chines giant to be listed. It cited its advantageous placement in a nation in which e-commerce is fast becoming a way of life, as Chinese consumers turn to the Internet to buy innumerable items. But Alibaba's prospectus cited statistics showing that the market hasn't been fully tapped. Just 45. 8 percent of China's population used the Internet, while 49 percent of customers shopped online.

Often described as a combination of eBay and Amazon, Alibaba handled $ 240 billion of merchandise in 2013. With more than 7 million merchants, it has more than $ 2 billion in revenue and profit of more than $ 1 billion. Alibaba's sheer size could weigh on the stock price of US rival Amazon if the Chinese company's shares are added to indexes and portfolios targeting e-commerce and related sectors.

Alibaba Group planned an initial public offering in the U. S., rather than Hong Kong, because the Hong Kong Stock Exchange disagree with the corporate governance structure of Alibaba, which is a partnership enterprises. Softbank took 36. 4% equity, while Yahoo took 24. 6% equity, Jack Ma (the entrepreneur) alone took 7%. The company is partnership structure of 28 founders and executives who will run the business when it is public. That approach bumped up against corporate governance rules of the Hong Kong Stock Exchange, which aim to give investors control over companies based on how many shares they own and limit so-called dual share-class structures.

Reference: Michael Barris. Alibaba files for IPO in US. http://usa.chinadaily.com.cn/business/2014-05/07/content_17490099. html;

Alibaba breaks off talks with the Hong Kong Stock Exchange after disagreement over corporate governance. http://www. usatoday. com/story/tech/2013/09/25/alibaba - ipo - us/2868651/

Extension Case: LDK listing in USA and Bankruptcy (2013)

LDK Solar is Chinese photovoltaics leader, which manufacture multicrystalline solar wafers of crystalline silicon material primarily made by slicing multicrystalline ingots or monocrystalline boules. Solar wafers are the principal raw material used to produce solar cells, which are devices capable of converting sunlight into electricity. In 2007, LDK offered 13 392 100 American depositary shares, or ADSs, and the selling shareholders identified in this prospectus are offering 3 991 900 ADSs. Each ADS represents one ordinary share, par value $ 0. 10 per share. The initial public offering price of the ADSs was between $ 25. 00 and $ 27. 00 per ADS.

But in 2013, LDK Solar is headed for bankruptcy, due to its immense debt burden and a global downturn in the solar energy market. Bankruptcy rumors have plagued LDK in recent months, causing investors to seek to divest themselves of shares in the company and regional clients to suspend orders for the company's products. Since the start of 2012, with management heavily regretting its decision to invest in LDK in 2011, just prior to the solar energy market entering a slump after riding an unprecedented wave of growth. LDK's 2011 Q4 financial report indicates that the company is mired in debt of U. S. $ 6 billion, and that annual interest payments alone amount to between $ 200 million and $ 300 million. Total Q4 losses were $ 589 million, marking the company's third successive losing quarter.

This is a dramatic turnaround for LDK, which until recently was a leader in the Chinese solar energy sector, and whose 37 year-old chairman Peng Xiaofeng was once feted as an industry wunderkind. Peng was one of the youngest and wealthiest figures in China's flourishing solar power sector, and LDK was for a brief period the world's largest producer of photovoltaic multi-crystalline silicon. LDK was also the first company from Jiangxi province to be listed on a U. S. stock exchange, and the province's second largest source of tax revenue. The company's ambitious high-debt growth model made LDK highly vulnerable to market vicissitudes, however, and the recent industry downturn may have done irreparable damage to the company's prospects. Despite the company's woes, Peng has put on a confident front for both the media and investors, taking the stage earlier this month at a banquet for business partners and customers held in a five-star hotel in Shanghai's financial district. In an interview with Nanfang Zhoumo, Peng dismissed the concerns of analysts by saying that "they have never seen a great company" and compared LDK's troubles to those encountered by Apple's Steve Jobs a decade ago.

Reference:

Marc Kenneth Howe. Bankruptcy Fears for China's LDK Solar Due to Market Downturn. http://www.renewableenergyworld.com/rea/news/article/2012/05/bankruptcy-fears-for-chinas-ldk-solar-due-to-market-downturn

Extended Reading and Online Practices:

1. The different listing criteria and corporate governance requirements among New York Stock Exchange (NYSE), Hong Kong Stock Exchange and NASDAQ.

2. Visit the website of Morgan Stanley www.morganstanleychian.com, learn the key points of becoming a listed company.

3. Visit the website of International Finance Corporation (IFC) www.ifc.org, which is a member of World Bank to promote sustainable private sector investment in developing countries as a way to reduce poverty and improve people's lives.

4. Visit the website of World Bank Group, www.worldbank.org, one of the world's largest sources of development assistance, work in more than 100 developing economies, bring a mix of finance and ideas to improve living standards and eliminate the worst forms of poverty.

5. Please discuss the fundamental documents in listing: PROSPECTUS（招股说明书）.

6. Please visit the website of NYSE Euronext（纽约—泛欧交易所集团） www.nyse.com, please compare with your partners the critical differences between NYSE and NYSE Euronext.

7. Many Chinese SMEs (small and medium enterprises) are attracted to be listed in OTCBB www.otcbb.com（Over the Counter Bulletin Board，美国场外柜台交易系统）. But now these companies are all in dilemma: Neither they can raise capital in OTCBB, Nor they

can upgrade to NYSE or Nasdaq. Could you find the roots of such dilemma today?

8. Since 2011, the Chinese listed companies in USA is in fad of exiting from American capital market, by contrast to the fad of listing in USA since 2002. 16 Chinese companies exited in 2011 and 25 companies exited in 2012, for example, Shanda (NASDAQ: SNDA), a leading interactive entertainment media company exited. Could you find reasons for the exit fad?

Case: KODA (Knock Out Discount Accumulator) 累积期权 —the Billionaire Killer

KODA is the short for Knock Out Discount Accumulator, is a kind of most complicated financial derivatives. The talented American investment bank invented such financial products. KODA is a kind of VAM (Valuation Adjustment Mechanism, 估值调整机制), or more frankly in Chinese is 对赌机制. That is why KODA in USA is called "I kill you later".

According to American Law, KODA is forbidden to sell in USA. In mainland China, in order to protect naivee investors from such mostcomplicated and risky KODA, it is forbidden to sell such products neither. It is interesting to see that American invented the product, but American authority prohibit and forbid to sell the product. In mainland China, to protect domestic products from such high risky financial derivatives, China forbid to sell and buy KODA.

But the greedy big name banks such as HSBC, Goldman Sachs, ABN Amro etc, used the legal loophole of Hong Kong which is an international free port and trap the domestic billionaire to open account in Hong Kong, and said KODA is juts a unique banking products with high return and little risks and fraud many billionaires use huge money to buy the products. The essence of KODA is kind of bet with the giant banks, but the success and gain possibility of naivee investors are very small, while the failure and loss possibility of naivee investors are huge and the incurring loss are UNLIMITED!

Extended Reading:

1. Watch on-line news: 汇丰银行兜售"金融鸦片", 国内富豪被亏没商量; http://v.jrj.com.cn/2010-05-14/000000013548.shtml

2. 累积看空期权 Accumulator 图解. http://news.hexun.com/2008-12-08/112110447.html

3. It is interesting and shocking to see that in recent years, the founder and entrepreneur of many companies are now fighting with their investors, so-called bloody capitalist. For example, NVC (雷士照明) and its investor Saif Fund (赛富基金) are in fierce fighting. How do you look at the root of their fight?

Discussion:

It is said that KODA and other complicated financial derivatives are kind of trapwhich cheat the financial naives. How do you think of this point of view?

Extended Reading Books:

1.

International Financial Markets (3rd edition), J. Orlin Grabbe;

2.

Capital Markets: Institutions and Instruments (6th edition), Peter S. Ross;

3. Joshua Rosenbaum, Joshua Pearl. *Investment Banking—Valuation, Leveraged Buyouts, and Mergers & Acquisitions*. John Wiley & Sons Press, 2009;

4. Please read WetFeet's industry profiles (www.wetfeet.com) of investment banking, mutual funds and brokerage, commercial banking, insurance, and accounting etc.

Online Lectures by Top University

1. Financial Markets (Yale University, 33 episodes)

Robert J. Shiller. http://open.163.com/special/financialmarkets/

2. Financial Theory (Yale University, 26 episodes)

John Geanakoplos. http://v.163.com/special/opencourse/financialtheory.html

3. Wall Street Internship (University of Pennsylvania, 6 episodes)

4. The Role of Global Capital Market（University of Melbourne，http://mooc.guokr.com/course/3651/The-Role-of-Global-Capital-Markets/

PART FIVE
The Strategy and Structure of International Business

CHAPTER 12
The Strategy of International Business

At the end of this chapter, you should be able to:

· Understand the concept, formulation and implementation of strategy;

· Understand how strategy correspond to environmental forces & corporate resources;

· How cost leadership strategy and differentiation strategy conflict and its solution;

· Be familiar with four basic strategies (international, multi-domestic, global and transnational strategies.

Case: Huawei Tunes Strategy to Stay Ahead in Europe (2013)

Huawei, the largest telecom solution provider in the world, achieved $ 40 billion sales revenue in 2013. For a company that is the epitome of China's manufacturing strength, Huawei has always managed to keep a low profile. But it is now giving the final touches to a strategy that it hopes will further consolidate and strengthen its presence in the highly innovative and demanding European market.

Huawei has just overtook its European rival Ericsson, which had a comparative figure of $ 35 billion in 2013. The company offers goods and services ranging from infrastructure to consumer handsets and has over 5 500 employees spread across several European countries. While its European headquarters is in Dusseldorf, it also has presence in countries such as France, Belgium, Holland, Poland, Romania, Spain and the UK. Leo Sun, chief executive of Huawei France and the man who is spearheading the European thrust, says Huawei will rely largely on its cutting edge in research and development (R&D) to help achieve its goals. Huawei have more than 18 000 patents and almost 50 percent of our employees are dedicated for R&D. In other words, huawei have the biggest R&D force in the world.

Huawei's efforts would be centered on tackling competition from rivals like Ericsson in the telecom sector, and others like Nokia, Siemens and Lucent in the network infrastructure market. But the company will take advantage of the opportunities in Europe to strengthen its presence in the enterprise and consumer sectors.

It is essential to integrate fully into the industrial environment for sustained long-term growth. For this it is also imperative to fully understand the European market, the regulatory environment and other social issues, need to develop common interests between the company and the society so that both can gain from the development. Most of Huawei's employees in Europe are Europeans. For example, Huawei France became the first Huawei subsidiary to be led by a European when the Frenchman Francoise Quentin became its chairman.

Strategically, these are all important areas that Huawei would like to get involved in the future in Europe. But most of the new domains the market is still not fully globalized. In the telecom sector, only the solutions provider domain is a globalized market. Because of globalization, competition is fierce and requires companies to be extremely innovative and customer- and client-oriented. So in the future, Huawei will adjust its strategy to build its consumer brand. This reflects Huawei's efforts to adjust its strategy and extend the reach of its innovative offerings from the telecom carrier network field to the enterprise and consumer fields. Its technicians and senior managers were also at the booth to help the visitors who want to experience the products. Many were fascinated by the state-of-the-art devices such as the recently unveiled Asend series of smart phones, including the four-core Ascend D Quad and the thin Ascend P1S. The innovation-driven company showed its strength with its capabilities across different fields such as telecom network equipment, corporate solutions and smart devices. Nevertheless, the company has yet to build an image as a fashionable chic brand. Huawei, which has grown rapidly over the past two decades to be the number two in telecom equipment market, tried to make adjustments to its strategies in order to find new growth drivers.

Reference: Huawei Tunes Strategy to Stay ahead in Europe. http://www.chinadaily.com.cn/cndy/2011-07/22/content_12956561.htm

Huawei adjusts strategy to build consumer brand. http://english.cri.cn/6826/2012/06/22/2021s707965.htm

Case: Haier: Innovation and Globalization Strategy (2005)

China acceded into the WTO on Dec. 11, 2002. In answering the call of new internalization trend, many Chinese companies went abroad only to retreat later to the old way of licensing agreements due to frustrating challenges. Haier decided that going abroad was not just for earning foreign exchange. More importantly, it was for creating China's own brands. Therefore, Haier came up with the "three-step strategy" of "going out, going in and going up". Acting on the idea of "taking on the more difficult ones first" Haier started by entering developed countries first to build a brand. Having done that, Haier took to the markets of developing countries with a much more advantageous position. In time, it created the localization mode of "three in one", combining design, manufacture and sales.

In this phase, Haier implemented a "Market Chain" management which was based on computer information systems and centered around order information flow, to drive logistics and capital flows and realize reengineering of business processes. This innovation on management system facilitated information flows within the enterprise, and encouraged employees to align their value orientation with the needs of users Haier's attempt to innovation and OBM policy attracts attention of Chinese and foreign media. Foreword: Haier's attempt and achievements in innovation and OBM policy has attracted attention of Chinese and foreign media. On November 27, 2005, the CCTV News broadcast a report, titled Haier: from Application to Preparation of Technical Criteria, on Haier's attempts and achievements in innovation and globalization practice. The article focuses upon Haier's innovative mechanism for R&D of Haier environmentally friendly dual-drive washing machine, saying that "Haier developed the dual-drive washing machine by integrating the resources of 8 departments, including Intellectual Property Rights, Marketing, R&D and After-sales Service, not only of the R&D, for development of the dual-drive washing machine and made breakthrough of 15 technical barriers and 32 patent inventions during 4 years, which is half the period length scheduled in advance."

For most consumers, the primary mode of thinking about Chinese manufacturers is not thinking about them at all. They are entities that linger off in the murky distance, behind a low price tag... Few think of Chinese firms as being innovative in the manner of a Toyota or a Samsung. But there is at least one Chinese company that has kept such models in mind as it has made its way into the American market. It is called Haier. In 2014, Haier achieved $ 30 billion sale revenues worldwide.

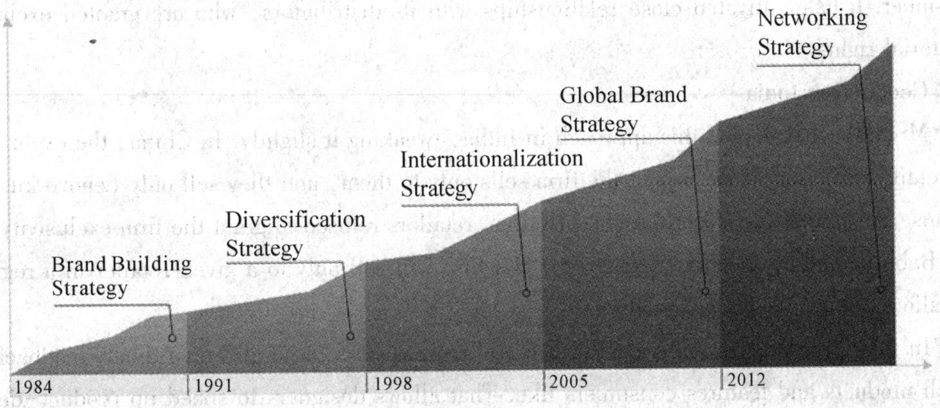

Reference: Haier: Innovation and globalization strategy. http://www.haier.com/EN/about_haier/news/201108/t20110817_52430.html

Case: How did Lenovo Become the World's Biggest Computer Company? (2013)

Lenovo (联想) started humbly, established in 1984 with $ 25 000 in a guard shack. It did well selling personal computers in China, but stumbled abroad. Its acquisition of IBM's PC business in 2005 led, according to one insider, "to nearly complete organ rejection". Gobbling up an entity double its size was never going to be easy. But cultural differences made it trickier. IBMers chafed at Chinese practices such as mandatory exercise breaks and public shaming of latecomers to meetings. Chinese staff, said a Lenovo executive at the time, marvelled that: "Americans like to talk; Chinese people like to listen. At first we wondered why they kept talking when they had nothing to say." Two Western chief executives failed to turn things around. By 2008, as the financial crisis raged, Lenovo was bleeding red ink.

Given all this, its recent success is startling. In the third quarter of 2012, Gartner, a consultancy, declared Lenovo the world's biggest seller of PCs, ahead of Hewlett-Packard (HP). Lenovo's rebound raises several questions. How did the firm recover from disaster? Is its new strategy sustainable? And does its rise signal the emergence of China's first world-class brand?

Lenovo's recovery owes much to a risky strategy, dubbed "Protect and Attack", embraced by the firm's current boss. After taking over in 2009, Yang Yuanqing moved swiftly. Keen to trim the bloat he inherited from IBM, Mr. Yang cut a tenth of the workforce. He then acted to protect its two huge profit centers—corporate PC sales and the China market—even as he attacked new markets with new products. When Lenovo bought IBM's corporate PC business, it was rumored to be a money-loser. Some whispered that Chinese ineptitude would sink IBM's well-regarded Think PC brand. Not so: shipments have doubled since the deal, and operating margins are thought to be above 5%. An even bigger profit centre is Lenovo's China business, which accounts for some 45% of total revenues. Amar Babu, who runs Lenovo's Indian business, thinks the firm's strategy in China offers lessons for other emerging markets. It has a vast distribution network, which aims to put a PC shop within 50km (30 miles) of nearly every consumer. It has cultivated close relationships with its distributors, who are granted exclusive territorial rights.

Conquering India

Mr. Babu has copied this approach in India, tweaking it slightly. In China, the exclusivity for retail distributors is two-way: the firm sells only to them, and they sell only Lenovo kit. But because the brand was still unproven in India, retailers refused to grant the firm exclusivity, so Mr. Babu agreed to one-way exclusivity. His firm will sell only to a given retailer in a region, but allows them to sell rival products.

In this way, Lenovo cultivates loyal brand ambassadors, who also give timely feedback on which products and features consumers like. That allows designers to speed up product-development cycles. The firm's first smartphone flopped, but paved the way for a flurry of hits.

Buoyed by success in corporate PCs and China, Lenovo has spent heavily to expand its share of the global PC market, especially in emerging markets. The brand is universally known in China; not so elsewhere. Spending on promotion, branding and marketing rose by \$ 248m in the year ending in March 2012 (though the firm will not reveal the full amount).

Acquisitions help, too. In 2011 Lenovo bought Medion, a European electronics firm, for \$ 738m, which doubled its share of the German PC market. The same year it spent \$ 450m to enter a joint venture with NEC that made it the largest PC firm inJapan. In 2012 it paid \$ 148m to buy CCE, Brazil's biggest computer firm. It is also opening factories in markets, including America, where it is surging.

To focus on PCs, Mr. Yang's predecessor sold Lenovo's smartphone arm for \$ 100m in 2008. Mr. Yang bought it back for twice as much the next year. He believes that PCs and other devices will converge, so knowledge of one area will breed expertise in the other. He may be right. Smartphone sales are red hot in China, and Lenovo is now selling mobiles and tablets in several emerging markets. Fourteen quarters in a row, Lenovo has grown faster than the overall PC industry, which shrank by 8% last quarter. A year and a half ago, the firm held double-digit PC market shares in a dozen countries; today, it does so in 34.

Alas, there is a tiny problem with Protect and Attack: the attack part is largely unprofitable. In most markets outside China, Lenovo's mobile phones, tablets and consumer PCs (as opposed to corporate sales of ThinkPads) lose money. "Profit is the long-term goal," says Mr. Yang, "but it helps to have a large revenue base." He vows to keep investing, regardless of returns, until the firm reaches a roughly 10% share in each of the target markets. Only with such scale is long-term profitability possible, he insists. Wong Waiming, the firm's chief financial officer, is confident Lenovo will eventually double its pretax profit margin of 2%. In 2009 Mr Yang persuaded the board to give him four years to show results. If allowed to invest, he promised to turn a $ 226m annual loss into a profit; in fact, the firm posted a profit of $ 164m last quarter. He vowed to lift annual revenues, then around $ 15 billion, past $ 20 billion; they are now $ 30 billion. He also said he would raise Lenovo's global market share from 7% to double digits; it is now close to 16%.

Lenovo does not simply churn out cheap goods. It is spending heavily on branding, distribution, manufacturing and product development. And alongside its cheap gizmos are many mid-range and some premium gadgets, such as the Yoga, a laptop that cleverly converts into a tablet. On January 6th, 2013, the firm announced a reorganisation: Lenovo Business Group will make things for cost-conscious consumers, while the new Think Business Group will chase the premium segment. Mr. Yang wants the Think brand to compete with Apple; he plans to open fancy showrooms like Apple's. Some credit must go to Liu Chuanzhi, the chairman of Legend Holdings, a Chinese investment firm from which Lenovo was spun out. Legend still holds a stake, but Lenovo shares trade freely in Hong Kong. Mr. Liu, one of those who schemed in the guard shack, has long dreamed that Legend Computer (as Lenovo was known until 2004) would become a global star.

Lenovo uses the hypercompetitive Chinese market as a test bed for products and strategies that are later rolled out globally. That is both a strength and a weakness. If Lenovo is to cement its market-share gains elsewhere, it must go beyond merely copying what works in China. Bad timing makes this problem more daunting. Lenovo has managed to get to the top of the PC mountain at precisely the moment when the mountain appears to be crumbling. Industry sales are shrinking as PCs are made obsolete by other devices. HP has even mooted quitting the business altogether. Some say Lenovo's costly global expansion will end in tears. Mr. Yang disagrees. Indeed, he shows an unfashionable faith in PCs, which are still 85% of Lenovo's revenues. They will keep evolving, he insists, citing the Yoga. Inventive firms can still profit from them. He gushes about a "PC+" approach, now being tried in China, that adds mobiles, tablets and smart televisions to PCs and connects them all with a local cloud. He also thinks Lenovo has a secret weapon. It has kept a lot of manufacturing in-house [why outsource to Foxconn (富士康) when you already pay Chinese wages?] Mr. Yang believes this in-house expertise gives his firm an edge in product development. But Lenovo must exploit that edge better than it has done so far if it is to compete with a technology powerhouse like Samsung and build a global brand anything like Apple's. If Lenovo is to become China's first world-class brand, it must come up with products that consumers are passionate about. In December, as he was honored as "Economic Figure of the Year" by China's national broadcaster, Mr. Yang described the task ahead for his firm and country: "My dream is that one day China will be more than a world factory… it will be a global centre for innovation."

Reference: Case: How did Lenovo become the world's biggest computer company? http://www.economist.com/news/business/21569398-how-did-lenovo-become-worlds-biggest-computer-compan

Discussion:

1. Haier act on the idea of "taking on the more difficult ones first", Haier started by entering developed countries first to build a brand. The strategy is by sharp contrast with Huawei who traditionally take the easiest one first, which means first enter developing countries and made a foothold, then consider to enter developed market. Please compare the internationalization strategy between Haier and Huawei.

2. Please discuss with your partners the basis of strategy formulation.

3. Visit the website of Lenovo www.lenovo.com.cn, learn more strategy in details about the company.

4. It is said that strategy is a Utopia, because strategy can be easily formulated by top executives, but it is most difficult to implement a strategy worldwide. How do you think the dilemma of strategy implementation?

5. Use the internet to find how the TNC s from home and abroad carry out business strategy in China?

Online Lectures by Top University:

1. Corporate Strategy (University of Illinois at Urbana, http://mooc.guokr.com/course/8129/Corporate-Strategy/)

2. Strategy Formulation (Copenhagen Business School, http://mooc.guokr.com/course/5831/Strategy-Formulation/)

3. Strategy Implementation (Copenhagen Business School, 教师: Nicolai Pogrebnyakov http://mooc.guokr.com/course/6051/Strategy-Implementation/)

CHAPTER 13
The Structure of International Business

At the end of this chapter, you should be able to:

· Understand the whole concept of organizational architecture;

· Understand the four differentorganizational choices of TNSs;

· Compare world product division& World area division;

· Understand the dilemma of Matrix structure;

· Know how the structure correspond to its strategy;

· Compare centralization &Decentraloization.

Case: Dual-Structure of TNCs in China: Conflicts and Dilemma

It is unique worldwide that TNCs employ dual-structure in China.

In the past, mainland business made limited contribution to whole company, for example, many years, the sales revenue of Microsoft China even fall behind of Microsoft Argentine, so that the conflicts were concealed. But with the rising status of mainland China business and the majority sales revenue from mainland China, together with the shrinking share of Hong Kong and Taiwan markets, the top executives from Beijing, became impatient and couldn't tolerate a guy from Hong Kong. Recently, more and more TNCs realized this had brought great harm to the company as a whole, and strove to make organizational reform on this dual-structure. Good news is that TNCs generally will enhance the status of Beijing executives and decentralize more power to Beijing office.

Discussion:

1. Please discuss the roots and effects of dual-structure in China.

2. Why some TNCs prefer decentralize power and enhance the status of subsidiaries worldwide, while others TNCs prefer centralize power in headquarters in home country?

Extended Reading Book:

体验微软. Gao Qunyao, the ex-CEO of Microsoft China.

Case: Matrix: From the Best to Give-up

An organizational structure defines how activities such as task allocation, coordination and supervision are directed towards the achievement of organizational aims. It can also be considered as the viewing glass or perspective through which individuals see their organization and its environment.

The matrix structure groups employees by both function and product. This structure can combine the best of both separate structures. A matrix organization frequently uses teams of employees to accomplish work, in order to take advantage of the strengths, as well as make up for the weaknesses, of functional and decentralized forms. An example would be a company that produces two products, "product A" and "product B". Using the matrix structure, this company would organize functions within the company as follows: "product A" sales department, "product A" customer service department, "product A" accounting, "product B" sales department, "product B" customer service department, "product B" accounting department. Matrix structure is amongst the purest of organizational structures, a simple lattice emulating order and regularity demonstrated in nature.

Matrix have both advantages and disadvantages; some of the disadvantages are an increase in the complexity of the chain of command. This occurs because of the differentiation between functional managers and project managers, which can be confusing for employees to understand who is next in the chain of command. An additional disadvantage of the matrix structure is higher manager to worker ratio that results in conflicting loyalties of employees. However the matrix structure also has significant advantages that make it valuable for companies to use. The matrix structure improves upon the "silo" critique of functional management in that it diminishes the vertical structure of functional and creates a more horizontal structure which allows the spread of information across task boundaries to happen much quicker. Moreover matrix structure allows for specialization that can increase depth of knowledge & allows individuals to be chosen according to project needs. This correlation between individuals and project needs is what produces the concept of maximizing strengths and minimizing weaknesses.

Top TNCs such as IBM uphold Matrix organizational architecture in 1990s. At that time, matrix is a fad and TNCs were proud of this stiff organization. But matrix suffered difficult time during late 1990s. Nowadays, Most TNCs abandoned matrix.

Reference: http://en.wikipedia.org/wiki/Organizational_structure

Discussion:

1. How did matrix bring conflicts between the global product department and the global area department?

2. Could you propose some initiative suggestions which can enhance the performance of matrix structure?

Extended Reading:

1. Jay R. Galbraith. *Designing Matrix Organization That Actually Works.*

2. Watch online interview of Chen Yaocang (陈耀昌), the ex-CEO of Walmart China. http://www.letv.com/ptv/vplay/1049845.html

Extended Reading: GIE (Global Integrated Enterprise)

—Discuss How IMB Saved 45 Billion USD

In 2006, Louis V. Gerstner, Jr. (郭士纳), the chairman and CEO of IBM proposed an innovative concept: GIE (Global Integrated Enterprise). From 2005 to 2011, during the six years, IBM successfully save cost of 45 billion USD.

In the 1990s, IBM experienced the most difficult time of its more than 100 years history: shrinking market share, up-soaring loss and burdensome inside bureaucracy... The once Blue Giant was thought by Bill Gates etc. that IBM is at the end of its business. But IMB finally survive and gain recovery.

Louis V. Gerstner initiated a series of strategic reforms in IBM, one most important reforms include: moving IBM from traditional organizational structure to newly initiated GIE model; setting up Global-sharing Service Centers. For example, IBM united diffused facilities and business worldwide , and united them into only 3 to 4global-sharing Service Centers which are responsible for global sourcing, finance and accounting, human resource management etc. In the six years from 2005 to 2011, every year IMB saved 7. 5 billion USD and six years 45 billion total.

In 1993 for example, in Europe alone, IBM owns 142 different accounting systems, different definition of key concept, different rules, different strategy... the accounting and financial departments of whole company is like a labyrinth, completely diffused dispersive worldwide. Accounting data can't realize the consistency and transparency among the subsidiaries.

And the relevant VIP customers info can't be shared among various subsidiaries. At that time, IBM employees exceed 14 000, twice the number of IBM's main competitors.

GIE is implemented through setting up Global Payment Center in Shanghai and Global Sourcing Center in Shenzhen, China. Global Finance Center in Kuala Lumpur, Malaysia and Global Human Resource Management Center in Manila, Philippines, the Global Assistance Center and Global Customer Service Center in Brisbane, Australia. These global centers did unify the dispersive worldwide business and procedures and realized integrated operation.

For example, under the GIE framework, the sourcing centers were reduced from 300 to 3, through global massive-scale integrated souring and procurement, every year 7. 5 billion USD is saved.

But implementing GIE is a most challenging and require all the executives and staffs are highly professional and skilled, and they must be ready to global communication and operation. For example, Mr. Rogerio Oliveira was appointed as the president of IBM Latin America in 2007, he was the president of IBM Brazil before. After the position promotion, the work tasks are completely different and challenges soar. For another example, the staffs working in the Global Customer Service Center in Brisbane, Australia will face IBM customers from worldwide, that means these staffs must work around the clock (24 hours a day) by 3 shifts every days and can speak different languages to ensure prompt and qualified services to IBM customers.

Reference: 曹子烈. 450 亿美元是这样节省的 http://www.ceconline.com/operation/ma/8800065464/02/

Discussion:

Please discuss the pros and cons of GIE. The great challenges GIE brings and how to deal with them.

Extended Reading Books: *Who Says Elephants Can't Dance*?

Online Lectures by Top University:

1. Introduction to Enterprise Architecture (Enterprise Architects, http://mooc.guokr.com/course/656/Introduction-to-Enterprise-Architecture/).

2. Designing the Organization: From Strategy to Organizational Structure (University of Illinois at Urbana-Champaign, University of Illinois at Urbana-Champaign).

CHAPTER 14
Entry Strategy and Alliance

At the end of this chapter, you should be able to:

- Be familiar with various entry modes;
- Understand the advantages and disadvantages of each entry mode;
- Understand the decision making framework of mode-selection;
- Indentify the factors which influence a firm's choice of entry mode;
- Know pros and cons of Greenfield & MA;
- Know strategic alliance emerging and evaluate its pros and cons.

Case: Airline Alliance

An airline alliance is an agreement between two or more airlines to cooperate on a substantial level. The three largest passenger airline alliances are Star Alliance, SkyTeam, and Oneworld. The Star Alliance, the largest and world first airline alliance, was founded in 1997, headquartered in Frankfurt, Germany. The Star Alliance urged competing airlines to form Oneworld in 1999 and SkyTeam in 2000.

Alliances also form between cargo airlines, such as that of WOW Alliance, SkyTeam Cargo, and ANA/UPS Alliance. Alliances provide a network of connectivity and convenience for international passengers and international packages. Alliances also provide convenient marketing branding to facilitate travelers making inter-airline codeshare connections within countries. This branding goes as far as to even include unified aircraft liveries among member airlines.

Reference: http://en.wikipedia.org/wiki/Airline_alliance

Discussion:

1. The emergence of various kinds ofalliance, the reason and its pros and cons.

Case: McDonald & KFC

With the development of China's economy, fast food from western countries are in a fad among Chinese customers. But concerning the two fast food tycoon from USA, namely the McDonald and KFC, their fate are quite different.

McDonald's is the leading global foodservice retailer with more than 35 000 local restaurants serving nearly 70 million people in more than 100 countries each day. By contrast, KFC

Corporation owns only 18 000 KFC outlets in 115 countries and territories around the world.

But that is just one part of the whole story, the McDonald china fall far behind of KFC in market share and number of stores. Kentucky Fried Chicken has been one of the most household international brands in urban China since it opened its first Western-style quick service restaurant in Beijing in 1987. KFC is now the largest fried chicken restaurant company in the world. While KFC McDonald's and Yum are still the largest fast food chains in China but, despite heavy investment, McDonald's has seen its market share by value stagnate at 2.3 percent since 2007.

What happened? First, let's examine the entry time of the two companies: KFC entered China in 1987 while McDonald in 1990, three years behind. What's more, KFC also did intensive market research on Chinese market and finally to be the first mover into China; while McDonald is just a follow-up rivals. Second, the entry mode: 80% of McDonald restaurants worldwide are franchised. But when entering China, McDonald became prudent and stick to whole-owned subsidiaries and set up high barriers and criteria for potential franchisee. In contrast, KFC from the beginning (1993) are enthusiastic about franchise mode, and in 2000, KFC even use Not-from -zero mode (“不从零开始”的特许经营模式). This means that the franchisee is not scratching from zero, but KFC will leave a ready-mature-profitable restaurant for the qualified franchisee.

What's more, KFC aims China as the most promising market and succeeds in its localization strategies in the huge China market. The most prominent success of KFC in China is not only the outcome of KFC's persistent tenets "quality, service and cleanliness" but also the achievements of its keen perception of cross-cultural marketing and its understanding of Chinese culture. The process of KFC's entry into China's market and its localization strategies towards China are two key factors of its great success in China.

Reference: www.kfc.com;

www. http://www.aboutmcdonalds.com;

KFC's Localization Strategies in China. http://blog.lidan.net/kfcs-localization-strategies-in-china/

Extended Reading: Franchising

Franchising is the practice of leasing for a prescribed period of time the right to use a firm's successful business model and brand. The word "franchise" is of Anglo-French derivation—from franc, meaning free—and is used both as a noun and as a (transitive) verb. For the franchisor, the franchise is an alternative to building "chain stores" to distribute goods that avoids the investments and liability of a chain. The franchisor's success depends on the success of the franchisees. The franchisee is said to have a greater incentive than a direct employee because he or she has a direct stake in the business.

Essentially, and in terms of distribution, the franchisor is a supplier who allows an operator, or a franchisee, to use the supplier's trademark and distribute the supplier's goods. In return, the operator pays the supplier a fee. Thirty three countries—including the United States and Australia—have laws that explicitly regulate franchising, with the majority of all other countries having laws which have a direct or indirect impact on franchising

The following U. S. listing tabulates the early 2010 ranking of major franchises along with the number of sub-franchisees (or partners). As can be seen from the names of the franchises, the United States is a leader in franchising, a position it has held since the 1930s when it used the approach for fast-food restaurants, food inns and, slightly later, motels at the time of the Great Depression. As of 2005, there were 909 253 established franchised businesses, generating $ 880.9 billion of output and accounting for 8.1 percent of all private, non-farm jobs. This amounts to 11 million jobs, and 4.4 percent of all private sector output.

1. Subway (sandwiches and salads) | startup costs $ 84 300–$ 258 300 (22 000 partners worldwide in 2004).

2. McDonald's | startup costs in 2010, $ 995 900–$ 1 842 700 (37 300 partners in 2010).

3. 7-Eleven Inc. (convenience stores) | startup costs in 2010 $ 40 500–$ 775 300, (28 200 partners in 2004).

4. Hampton Inns & Suites (midprice hotels) | startup costs in 2010 $ 3 716 000–$ 15 148 800.

5. Great Clips (hair salons) | startup costs in 2010 $ 109 000 – $ 203 000.

6. H&R Block (tax preparation and now e-filing) | startup costs $ 26 427–$ 84 094 (11 200 partners in 2004).

7. Dunkin' Donuts | startup costs in 2010 $ 537 750–$ 1 765 300.

8. Jani-King (commercial cleaning) | startup costs $ 11 400–$ 35 050, (11 000 partners worldwide in 2004).

9. Servpro (insurance and disaster restoration and cleaning) | startup costs in 2010 $ 102 250–$ 161 150.

10. MiniMarkets (convenience store and gas station) | startup costs in 2010 $ 1 835 823–$ 7 615 065.

Mid-sized franchises like restaurants, gasoline stations and trucking stations involve substantial investment and require all the attention of a businessperson. There are also large franchises like hotels, spas and hospitals, which are discussed further undertechnological alliances.

Three important payments are made to a franchisor: (a) a royalty for the trademark, (b) reimbursement for the training and advisory services given to the franchisee, and (c) a percentage of the individual business unit's sales. These three fees may be combined in a single "management" fee. A fee for "disclosure" is separate and is always a "front-end fee".

A franchise usually lasts for a fixed time period (broken down into shorter periods, which each require renewal, and serves a specific territory or geographical area surrounding its location. One franchisee may manage several such locations. Agreements typically last from five to thirty years, with premature cancellations or terminations of most contracts bearing serious consequences for franchisees. A franchise is merely a temporary business investment involving renting or leasing an opportunity, not the purchase of a business for the purpose of ownership. It is classified as a wasting asset due to the finite term of the license.

Franchise fees are on average 6.7% with an additional average marketing fee of 2%. A franchise can be exclusive, non-exclusive or "sole and exclusive". Although franchisor revenues and profit may be listed in a franchise disclosure document (FDD), no laws require an estimate of franchisee profitability, which depends on how intensively the franchisee "works" the franchise. Therefore, franchisor fees are typically based on "gross revenue from sales" and not on profits realized. See remuneration.

Various tangibles and intangibles such as national or international advertising, training and other support services are commonly made available by the franchisor. Franchise brokers help franchisors find appropriate franchisees. There are also main 'master franchisors' who obtain the rights to sub-franchise in a territory. According to the International Franchise Association approximately 4% of all businesses in the United States are franchisee-worked.

Reference: http://en.wikipedia.org/wiki/Franchising

Discussion:

1. Visit the websites of KF and McDonald to study their strategy formulation and strategy implementation in details.

2. The startup cost of McDonald's in 2010 is around \$ 995 900-\$ 1 842 700 (37 300 partners in 2010) which is about 8 million RMB minimum... By contrast, That of KFC is about 2 million RMB. Please compare their entry barriers and its effects.

3. Discuss the prons and cons of KFC's Not-from -zero mode ("不从零开始"的特许经营模式).

Online Lectures by Top University:

1. International Marketing Entry and Execution (Yonsei University, http://mooc.guokr.com/course/7328/International-Marketing-Entry-and-Execution/)

tion. One franchisee may manage several such locations. Agreements typically last from five to thirty years, with premature cancellations or terminations of most contracts bearing serious consequences for franchisees. A franchise is merely a temporary business investment involving renting or leasing an opportunity, not the purchase of a business for the purpose of ownership. It is classified as a wasting asset due to the finite term of the license.

Franchise fees are on average 6.7% with an additional average marketing fee of 2.6%. A franchise can be exclusive, non-exclusive or "sole and exclusive". Although franchisor revenues and profit may be listed in a franchise disclosure document (FDD), no laws require an estimate of franchisee profitability, which depends on how intensively the franchisee "works" the franchise. Therefore, franchisor fees are typically based on "gross revenue from sales" and not on profits realized. See remuneration.

Various tangibles and intangibles such as national or international advertising, training and other support services are commonly made available by the franchisor. Franchise brokers help franchisors find appropriate franchisees. There are also main "master franchisees" who obtain the rights to sub-franchise in a territory. According to the International Franchise Association approximately 4% of all businesses in the United States are franchise-worked.

Reference: http://en.wikipedia.org/wiki/Franchising

Discussion:

1. Visit the websites of KFC and McDonald's to study their strategy formulation and strategy implementation in details.

2. The startup cost of McDonald's in 2010 is around $ 995,900—$ 1,842,700 (+ $ 27,500 partners in 2010) which is about 8 million RMB minimum. By contrast, that of KFC is about 2 million RMB. Please compare their entry barriers and its effects.

3. Discuss the pros and cons of KFC's non-from-zero mode (不从零开始加盟模式).

Online Lectures by Top University

1. International Marketing: Entry and Execution (Cornell University)

http://www.coursera.org/course/International-Marketing-Entry-and-Execution

PART SIX
International Business Operations

CHAPTER 15
Exporting, Importing and Countertrade

At the end of this chapter, you should be able to:

· Export and its pros and cons;

· Understand government's role in export-promotion;

· The on-filed export operation andtactics in China;

· How a manager can improve his firm's export performance;

· Understand the emerging of countertrade and its pros and cons.

Case: China Restart Barter Trade of Petroleum (2007)

Barter, the direct exchange of goods or services—without an intervening medium of exchange or money—either according to established rates of exchange or by bargaining. It is considered the oldest form of commerce. Barter is common among traditional societies, particularly in those communities with some developed form of market. Goods may be bartered within a group as well as between groups, although gift exchange probably accounts for most intragroup trade, particularly in small and relatively simple societies.

China is No. 2 petroleum importer worldwide, just after USA. In 2013, China imported 282 million tons. About 60% of domestic petroleum oil consumption is imported. But the price of international petroleum is most volatile, For example, in 2007, with soar of international petroleum price, China decided to embark on the oldest trade form again in 2007. Yangpu Barter Exchange (洋浦易货交易所), as the first barter exchange, was set up in Yangpu Economic Development Zone in March 2006. The main controlling shareholders are Yangpu Bisheng Industrial Co., Bisheng International Group, Huayi Jinxuan Entrepreneur Center.

The potential members of Yangpu Barter Exchange include Africa Petroleum Countries, Middle East Petroleum Countries, Southern American countries, Russia etc. Especially nowadays, African countries are carrying out heavy infrastructure construction so that barter trade with these African petroleum countries are most promising. Further more, on April 10, 2012, China signed barter trade agreement with Thailand and use Chinese vegetables to exchange Thai's petroleum.

Reference: 中国 2007 年启动国际石油易货贸易. http://oil.in-en.com/html/oil-20062006072024787.html

Discussion：

Please discuss the background of barter trade boom, the benefits and costs of such barter agreement.

Case：China Factories Suffered from Export Fall（2014）

Since the financial crisis started in 2008, world economy is stagnant and the demand in China main markets slowing sharply. China's weaker than expected trade numbers were being stomached by industrialists in the export hub of the Pearl River Delta, who are seeing an uptick in orders but don't see any lasting recovery till next year.

In China's manufacturing heartlands of the Pearl River Delta, the financial crisis has devastated thousands of export-oriented factories unable to cope with the twin blows of plunging Western orders and a trend of rising labour and production costs. Ttrade numbers were weaker than expected. The lean times were evident at the Silver Bright Footwear Factory in Dongguan's gritty Tangxia town, where several of its 100-metre long production lines remained idle. But a stream of pink baby shoes for U. S. brand NEXT and flashy urban-fashion trainers for Japan's BAPE were making their way down other factory belts as workers stitched and glued shoes in steadily growing numbers given a mild rise in Western demand.

The Shenzhen special economic zone has been China's leading export area for years running. It and other cities in Guangdong's Pearl River delta manufacturing heartland account for one-third of the country's exports, the vast majority of which are assembled by migrant laborers. Three-quarters of Shenzhen's official population of 8. 6m lack the "permanent residency" status that would entitle them to full medical and education benefits. In 2008, on the 30th anniversary of China's reform era, Shenzhen stands on the verge of another metamorphosis as exporters in low-end, labor-intensive sectors fall by the wayside. Which means Shenzhen must transform again?

Reference：James Pomfret. C. hina factories shrug off May export fall on nascent orders. http://cn.reuters.com/article/companyNews/idUKHKG5175220090611? symbol=0551. HK

China's export fall means Shenzhen must transform again. http://www.ftchinese.com/story/001023662/en

Extended Reading：Tax Refund in China

China adopted export tax refund early in 1984. During 2003 to 2012, China accumulate export tax refund up to 5. 3 Billion RMB, tax refund played an very import role which helped China become No. 1 exporter worldwide.

Export tax refund is inline with international practice and the principle of mutual benefit and reciprocity. For example, the VAT paid for the purchase of export goods in the Chinese market, or for purchases used in the manufacture of export goods, can be refunded in whole or in part, given that the following requirements are satisfied：

1. The goods are subject to VAT or consumption taxes under the Chinese tax rules;

2. The nature of the export transaction must be treated as sales, not the disposal of fixed assets, in the books of accounts for the exporter;

3. The goods must have physically left the country (except for that shipped to export processing zones);

4. The exporter has to produce evidence showing that the foreign exchange

Reference: An Introduction to VAT Export Refund Rules in China www.china-tax.net

Discussion:

Please discuss with your partners the slack situation of China export.

Extended Reading and Online Practices:

1. Visit the website of Ministry of Commerce www.mofcom,gov.cn, and learn more data and info about China export and import.

2. Visit the website of General Administration of Customs of PRC www.customs.gov.cn, learn customs practices and info.

3. Visit the website of State Administration of Foreign Exchange (SAFE) www.safe.gov.cn, learn export financial verification (出口收付汇核销).

4. Visit the website of China Port (中国电子口岸) www.chinaport.gov.cn/kfzq/cjwt/ckts, learn the refund tax policy of China and its practices.

Extended Reading: Export Hands-on Experiences

Export is a most complicated business practices with long procedures, heavy documents, high risks and skills-demanding. But remember always sell as close to the market as possible. The fewer intermediaries one has the better, because every intermediary needs some percentage for his share in his business, which means less profit for the exporter and higher prices for the customer. All goods for export must be efficiently produced. They must be produced with due regard to the needs of export markets. It is no use trying to sell windows which open outwards in a country where, traditionally, windows open inwards.

The basic procedures include: Selecting the markets, Selecting the company, Making effective business correspondence, Selecting prospective buyers, Selecting channels of distribution, Negotiating with prospective buyers, Processing an export order, Entering into export contract, Export pricing and costing, Understanding risks in international trade.

Export suffer various kinds of risks, for example, Credit risk, Currency risk, Carriage risk, Country risk etc. These risks can be insured to a great extent by taking appropriate steps. Credit risk against the buyer can be covered by insisting upon an irrevocable letter of credit from the overseas buyer. An appropriate policy from Export Credit and Guarantee Corporation can be obtained for this purpose. Country risks are also covered by the ECGC. As regards currency risk, i. e. possible loss due to adverse fluctuation in exchange rate. You should obtain forward cover from your bank authorised to deal in foreign exchange. Alternatively, you should obtain export order in Indian rupee. Carriage risk, i. e. possible loss of cargo in transit can be covered by taking a marine insurance policy from the general insurance companies.

Dispatching Samples

As the overseas buyers generally insist for the samples before placing confirmed orders, it is essential that the samples are attractive, informative and have retention and reminder value. Besides, the exporter should know the Government policy and procedures for export of samples from India. He should also be aware about the cheapest modes of sending samples.

In this connection, it is advised that the postal channel is comparatively cheaper than sending samples by air. While sending samples through postal channel due regard should be given to weight and dimension of the post parcels as postal authorities have prescribed maximum weight and dimension for the post parcels handled by them. Where it is not possible to send the samples by post parcels, the same may be sent by air. So far as the Government policy regarding export of samples is concerned, distinction has been made between export of commercial samples and gift parcels. You need consult the tariff schedule of the target country

Appointing Agents

Selling through an overseas agent is an effective strategy. These agents serve as a source of market intelligence. Regularly sending the latest trends on the current fashion, taste and price in the market. Being a man on the spot, the agent is in a position to render his advice to exporter or new methods and strategy for pushing up sales of your products. He also provides you support in the matter of transportation, reservation of accommodation, appointment with the government as and when required by you. In some countries it is compulsory under their law to sell through local agents only. It is, therefore, essential that you should carefully select your overseas agent.

Consider the points listed below when appointing an Agent: Size of the agent's company; Date of foundation of the agent's company; Company's ownership and control; Company's capital, funds, available and liabilities; Name, age and experience of the company's senior executives; Number, age and experience of the company's salesman; Other agencies that the company holds, including those of competing products and turn-over of each; Length of company's association with other principal; New agencies that the company obtained or lost during the past year; Company's total annual sales and the trends in its sales in recent years; Company's sales coverage, overall and by area; Number of sales calls per month and per salesman by company staff; Any major obstacles expected in the company's sales growth; Agent's capability to provide sales promotion and advertising services; Agent's transport facilities and warehousing capacity; Agent's rate of commission; payment terms required.

References on the agents from banks, trade associations and major buyers; Some source of information on agents are: Government Departments Trade Associations; Chambers of Commerce; Banks; Independent Consultants; Export Promotion Councils; Advertisement Abroad.

Acquire Export License

Exports free unless regulated. Application for an Export License: An application for grant of export license in respect of items mentioned.

Acquire Export Credit Insurance

Export credit insurance protects you from the consequences of the payment risks, both political and commercial. It enables you to expand your overseas business without fear of loss. Further, it creates a favorable climate for you under which you can hope to get timely and liberal credit facilities from the banks at home.

You can obtain Export Credit Insurance from the Export Credit and Guarantee Corporation.

Arranging Finance

Financial assistance to the exporters are generally provided by Commercial Banks, before shipment as well as after shipment of the said goods. The assistance provided before shipment of goods is known as per-shipment finance and that provided after the shipment of goods is known as post-shipment finance. Pre-shipment finance is given for working capital for purchase of raw-material, processing, packing, transportation, ware-housing etc. of the goods meant for export. Post-shipment finance is provided for bridging the gap between the shipment of goods and realization of export proceeds. The later is done by the Banks by purchasing or negotiating the export documents or by extending advance against export bills accepted on collection basis. While doing so, the Banks adjust the pre-shipment advance, if any, already granted to the exporter.

Pre-Shipment Finance

An application for pre-shipment advance should be made by you to your banker along with the following documents: Confirmed export order/contract or L/C etc. in original. Where it is not available, an undertaking to the effect that the same will be produced to the bank within a reasonable time for verification and endorsement should be given. An undertaking that the advance will be utilised for the specific purpose of procuring/manufacturing/shipping etc., of the goods meant for export only, as stated in the relative confirmed export order or the L/C. If you are a sub-supplier and want to supply the goods to the Export/Trading/Star Trading House or Merchant Exporter, an undertaking from the Merchant. Any other document required by the Bank.

Following special schemes are also available in respect of pre-shipment finance:

EXIM Bank's scheme for grant of foreign currency pre-shipment credit to exporters for financing cost of imported inputs for manufacture of export products.

Scheme of export packing credit to sub-suppliers from export order.

Packing credit for deemed exports.

Post Shipment Finance

Post-shipment finance is the finance provided against shipping documents. It is also provided against duty drawback claims. It is provided in the following forms:

Purchase of Export Documents drawn under Export Order: Purchase or discount facilities in respect of export bills drawn under confirmed export order are generally granted to the customers who are enjoying Bill Purchase/Discounting limits from the Bank. As in case of purchase or discounting of export documents drawn under export order, the security offered under L/C by way of substitution of credit-worthiness of the buyer by the issuing bank is not available, the bank financing is totally dependent upon the credit worthiness of the buyer, i. e. the importer, as well as that of the exporter or the beneficiary. The documents dawn on DP basis are parted with through foreign correspondent only when payment is received while in case of DA bills documents (including that of title to the goods) are passed on to the overseas importer against the acceptance of the draft to make payment on maturity. DA bills are thus unsecured. The bank financing against export bills is open to the risk of non-payment. Banks, in order to enhance security, generally opt for ECGC policies and guarantees which are issued in favor of the exporter/banks to protect their interest on percentage basis in case of non-payment or delayed payment which is not on account of mischief, mistake or negligence on the part of exporter. Within the total limit of policy issued to the customer, drawee-wise limits are generally fixed for individual customers. At the time of purchasing the bill bank has to ascertain that this drawee limit is not exceeded so as to make the bank ineligible for claim in case of non-payment.

Advances against Export Bills Sent on Collection: It may sometimes be possible to avail advance against export bills sent on collection. In such cases the export bills are sent by the bank on collection basis as against their purchase/discounting by the bank. Advance against such bills is granted by way of a "separate loan" usually termed as "post-shipment loan". This facility is, in fact, another form of post- shipment advance and is sanctioned by the bank on the same terms and conditions as applicable to the facility of Negotiation/Purchase/Discount of export bills. A margin of 10 to 25% is, however, stipulated in such cases. The rates of interest etc., chargeable on this facility are also governed by the same rules. This type of facility is, however, not very popular and most of the advances against export bills are made by the bank by way of negotiation/purchase/discount.

Advance against Goods Sent on Consignment Basis: When the goods are exported on consignment basis at the risk of the exporter for sale and eventual remittance of sale proceeds to him by the agent/consignee, bank may finance against such transaction subject to the customer enjoying specific limit to that effect. However, the bank should ensure while forwarding shipping documents to its overseas branch/correspondent to instruct the latter to deliver the document only against Trust Receipt/Undertaking to deliver the sale proceeds by specified date, which should be within the prescribed date even if according to the practice in certain trades a bill for part of the estimated value is drawn in advance against the exports.

Advance against Undrawn Balance: In certain lines of export it is the trade practice that bills are not to be drawn for the full invoice value of the goods but to leave small part undrawn for payment after adjustment due to difference in rates, weight, quality etc. to be ascertained after approval and inspection of the goods. Banks do finance against the undrawn balance if undrawn balance is in conformity with the normal level of balance left undrawn in the particular line of export subject to a maximum of 10% of the value of export and an undertaking is obtained from the exporter that he will, within 6 months from due date of payment or the date of shipment of the goods, whichever is earlier surrender balance proceeds of the shipment.

Advance against Retention Money: Banks also grant advances against retention money, which is payable within one year from the date of shipment, at a concessional rate of interest up to 90 days. If such advances extend beyond one year, they are treated as deferred payment advances which are also eligible for concessional rate of interest.

Advances against Claims of Duty Drawback: Duty Drawback is permitted against exports of different categories of goods. Drawback in relation to goods manufactured inIndia and exported means a rebate of duties chargeable on any imported materials or excisable materials used in manufacture of such goods. The claims of duty drawback are settled by Custom Bureau and local Tax Authorities.

Rates of Interest

The rate of interest depends on the nature of the Bills, i. e., whether it is a demand bill or usance bill. Like pre-shipment, post-shipment finance is also available at concessional rate of interest. Present rates of interest are as under:

FORFEITING FINANCE BY AUTHORISED DEALERS

The authorised dealers (Banks) to arrange forfeiting of medium term export receivables on the same lines as per the scheme of EXIM Bank and many International forfeiting agencies. Forfeiting may be usefully employed as an additional window of export finance particularly for exports to those countries for which normal exports credit is not intended by the commercial banks. It must be noted that charges of forfaiting are eventually to be passed on to the ultimate buyer and should, therefore, be so declared on relative export declaration forms.

EXIM BANK FINANCE

Besides commercial banks, export finance is also made available by the EXIM bank. The EXIM bank provides financial assistance to promote host country exports through direct financial assistance, overseas investment finance, term finance for export production and export development, pre-shipment credit, lines of credit, re-lending facility, export bills re-discounting, refinance to commercial banks, finance for computer software exports, finance for export marketing and bulk import finance to commercial banks. The EXIM Bank also extends non-funded facility to Indian exports in the form of guarantees. The diversified lending programme of the EXIM Bank now covers various stages of exports, i. e. from the development export markets to expansion of production capacity for exports, production for export and post shipment financing. The EXIM Bank's focus is on export of manufactured goods, project exports, exports of technology, services and export of computer software.

Exporter initiates negotiations with the prospective overseas buyer with regard to the basic contract price, period of credit, rate of interest, etc. After successful negotiations, he furnishes the relevant particulars such as name and country of overseas buyer, contract value, nature of goods, tenure of credit, name and country of guaranteeing bankers to the Exim Bank and requests for an indicative discounting quote. Exim Bank obtains the indicative quote of forfeiting discount together with commitment fee and other charges, if any, to be paid by the exporter, from an overseas forfaiting agency. On receipt of the indicative quote from the Exim Bank, the exporter finalises the terms of the contract, loading the discount and other charges in the value and approaches Exim Bank for obtaining a firm quote. Exim Bank arranges to get the same from an appropriate overseas forfaiting agency and furnishes the same to the exporter. At this stage, exporter would be required to confirm acceptance of the arrangement to Exim Bank within a specific period as stipulated by that Bank.

The export contract clearly indicates that the overseas buyer shall prepare a series of avalised Promissory Notes in favour of the exporter and hand them over against the shipping documents to his banker. The Prommissory Notes will be endorsed with the words without recourse by the exporter and handed over to his banker inIndia for onward transmission to the Exim Bank.

Alternatively, the export contract may provide for exporter to draw a series of Bills of exchange on the overseas buyer which will be sent with the shipping documents through latter's banker for acceptance by the overseas buyer. Overseas buyer's banker will handover the documents against acceptance of Bills of Exchange by the buyer and signature of "aval" or the guaranteeing bank. Avalised and accepted bills of exchange will be returned to the exporter through his banker. Exporter will endorse avalised Bills of Exchange with the words 'without recourse' and return them to his banker for onward transmission to the Exim Bank. Exim Bank will forward the Bills of Exchange/Promissory Notes after verification to the forfaiting agency for discounting by the latter. Exim Bank will arrange to collect the discounted proceeds of Promissory Notes/Bills of Exchange from the overseas forfaiting agency and effect payment to the nostro account of the exporter's bank as per the latter's instruction.

International Success Tip: Specimen Copy of Agreement

An agreement made this the ________ day ________ of between ________ (name and address) hereinafter called the exporters of the first part and ________ (name and address) hereinafter called the importers of the second part, wherein the exporters grant to the importers the importation and selling right in the territory of ________ (fill name of country) for ________ (names and brief description of product) subject to the terms and conditions given below:

The exporter agrees that during the currency of the agreement he will not correspond or in any way deal with any part in the territory specified unless requested to do so by the importers.

The exporter agrees that any orders or enquiries relating to the specified territory received by him during the currency of this agreement will be passed on to the importers to deal with.

The exporter agrees that he will make shipment of all orders received from the importers by earliest shipping opportunity unless prevented from so doing by circumstances beyond the former's control.

The exporter agrees to charge the importers for all goods ordered during the currency of this agreement the prices detailed in Price List No. __________ appended to this agreement unless any order is received at least one month after notification of price changes by the exporter to the importer.

The exporter agrees to pay the importer commission on __________ (fill in the dates of each year during the currency of this agreement) at the rate of __________ per cent of __________ the F. O. B. value of all orders satisfactorily completed during the __________ months preceding the dates specified.

The exporter agrees that he will allow to the importers __________ per cent __________ of the value of all business satisfactorily completed with the importers during the currency of this agreement as contribution towards the importer's costs in publicising the products covered by this agreement. This allowance is to be settled by deduction from the manufacturer's invoices to the importers.

The importers agree that during the currency of this agreement they will not sell, recommend or in any other way deal with any competing or rivaling lines in the territory specified.

The importers agree that they will use their best efforts and endeavors at all times during the currency of this agreement to promote the sales of products covered by this agreement.

The importers agree that they will make net and full payment for all goods ordered through confirmed and irrevocable letter of credit established in __________ (name of manufacturer's town or city). OR The importers agree that they will make net and full payment for all goods ordered against presentation of draft and shipping documents in __________ (name of importer's town or city). OR The importers agree that they will immediately upon presentation at __________ and retire such drafts net and in full upon maturity.

The importers agree that they will write to the manufacturer at least once each calendar month and will send to the manufacturer a full market report on the prospects for sale of the products covered by this agreement every six months.

The importer agrees that they will place regular and adequate order with the manufacturer amounting in total to not less than __________ during the first calendar year and not less than Rs __________ in each and every subsequent year during the currency of this agreement.

This agreement shall become valid with effect from the date of shipment of the substantial order amounting in value of not less than Rs. __________ and remain in force for a period of twelve calendar months there from subject to either party being at liberty to terminate this agreement without notice in the event of the other party being in breach of any of the terms and conditions stated herein.

Notwithstanding anything herein aforesaid if during the first twelve calendar months the importers have placed satisfactory orders with the exporters amounting to not less than Rs __________ this agreement shall be automatically renewed year after year provided that in the twelve calendar months immediately preceding the expiry date satisfactorily business amounting in total to not less than Rs __________ has been placed by the importers with the manufacturer.

Any disputes arising under this agreement shall be settled in accordance with Indian Law in (__________)

Witness __________ (Exporter)

Witness __________ (Importer)

CHAPTER 16
Global Production, Outsourcing and Logistics

At the end of this chapter, you should be able to:

- Understand the whole concept of supply chainmanagement;
- Identify the main factors which influence the choice of global production;
- Discuss the pros and cons of virtual companies;
- Understand the decision-making framework concerning outsourcing;
- Understand the role global logistics and its challenges.

Case: Walmart: Keys to Successful Supply Chain Management

A supply chain is a system of organizations, people, activities, information, and resources involved in moving a product or service from supplier to customer. Supply chain activities transform natural resources, raw materials, and components into a finished product that is delivered to the end customer. In sophisticated supply chain systems, used products may re-enter the supply chain at any point where residual value is recyclable. Supply chains link value chains.

The case of Walmart demonstrates that a successful supply chain management strategy can lead to lower product costs and highly competitive pricing for the consumer.

Over the past ten years, Walmart has become the world's largest and arguably most powerful retailer with the highest sales per square foot, inventory turnover, and operating profit of any discount retailer. Walmart owes its transition from regional retailer to global powerhouse largely to changes in and effective management of its supply chain.

Walmart began with the goal to provide customers with the goods they wanted when and where they wanted them. Walmart then focused on developing cost structures that allowed it to offer low everyday pricing. The key to achieving this goal was to make the way the company replenishes inventory the centerpiece of its strategy, which relied on a logistics technique known as cross docking. Using cross docking, products are routed from suppliers to Walmart's warehouses, where they are then shipped to stores without sitting for long periods of time in inventory. This strategy reduced Walmart's costs significantly and they passed those savings on to their customers with highly competitive pricing. Walmart then concentrated on developing a more highly structured and advancedsupply chain management strategy to exploit and enhance this competitive advantage.

Components of Supply Chain Management (SCM)

The main elements of a supply chain include purchasing, operations, distribution, and integration. The supply chain begins with purchasing. Purchasing managers or buyers are typically responsible for determining which products their company will sell, sourcing product suppliers and vendors, and procuring products from vendors at prices and terms that meets profitability goals.

Supply chain operations focus on demand planning, forecasting, and inventory management. Forecasts estimate customer demand for a particular product during a specific period of time based on historical data, external drivers such as upcoming sales and promotions, and any changes in trends or competition. Using demand planning to develop accurate forecasts is critical to effective inventory management. Forecasts are compared to inventory levels to ensure that distribution centers have enough, but not too much, inventory to supply stores with a sufficient amount of product to meet demand. This allows companies to reduce inventory carrying costs while still meeting customer needs.

Moving the product from warehouses or manufacturing plants to stores and ultimately to customers is the distribution function of the supply chain.

Supply chain integration refers to the practice of developing a collaborative workflow among all departments and components involved in the supply chain to maximize efficiencies and build a lean supply chain.

Walmart's Method of Managing the Supply Chain

Walmart has been able to assume market leadership position primarily due to its efficient integration of suppliers, manufacturing, warehousing, and distribution to stores. Its supply chain strategy has four key components: vendor partnerships, cross docking and distribution management, technology, and integration.

Walmart's supply chain begins with strategic sourcing to find products at the best price from suppliers who are in a position to ensure they can meet demand. Walmart establishes strategic partnerships with most of their vendors, offering them the potential for long-term and high volume purchases in exchange for the lowest possible prices.

Suppliers then ship product to Walmart's distribution centers where the product is cross docked and then delivered to Walmart stores. Cross docking, distribution management, and transportation management keep inventory and transportation costs down, reducing transportation time and eliminating inefficiencies.

Technology plays a key role in Walmart's supply chain, serving as the foundation of their supply chain. Walmart has the largest information technology infrastructure of any private company in the world. Its state-of-the-art technology and network design allow Walmart to accurately forecast demand, track and predict inventory levels, create highly efficient transportation routes, and manage customer relationships and service response logistics.

Benefits of Efficient Supply Chain Management

WalMart's supply chain management strategy has provided the company with several sustainable competitive advantages, including lower product costs, reduced inventory carrying costs, improved in-store variety and selection, and highly competitive pricing for the consumer. This strategy has helped Walmart become a dominant force in a competitive global market. As technology evolves, Walmart continues to focus on innovative processes and systems to improve its supply chain and achieve greater efficiency.

Reference: Walmart: Keys to Successful Supply Chain Management. http://www.usanfranonline.com/resources/supply-chain-management/walmart-keys-to-successful-supply-chain-management/

On-line Practice and Discussion:

Visit the website of Supply Chain Brain, www.supplychainbrain.com, an excellent web source from global logistics and supply chain management.

Extended Reading: Virtual Enterprise (虚拟企业)

The concept of Virtual Enterprise is first initiated by Kenneth Preiss, Steven L. Goldman, Roger N. Nage in 1991. A virtual enterprise (VE) is a temporary alliance of businesses that come together to share skills or core competencies and resources in order to better respond to business opportunities, and whose cooperation is supported by computer networks. It is a manifestation of distributed collaborative networks. A virtual enterprise is a particular case of virtual organization. Virtual enterprises have become increasingly common in the area of research and development, with often far-flung organizations forming alliances that amount to a "Virtual Research Laboratory".

The emergence of the virtual network enterprise represents a dynamic response to the crisis of the vertical bureaucracy type of business organization. However, its key performance criteria—interconnectedness and consistency—pose tremendous challenges as the completion of the distributed tasks of the network must be integrated across the barriers of missing face-to-face clues and cultural differences. The social integration of the virtual network involves the creation of identities of the participating nodes, the building of trust between them, and the sharing of tacit and explicit knowledge among them. The conventional organization already doing well in these areas seems to have an edge when going virtual.

Reference: Lauge Baungaard Rasmussen, Arne Wangel. Work in the virtual enterprise—creating identities, building trust, and sharing knowledge

Discussion: How do the virtual enterprises operate?

Extended Reading Books (见图):

Online Lectures by Top University：

Supply Chain Fundamentals：MITx MicroMaster's Credential in Supply Chain Management（MIT，http：//mooc.guokr.com/course/6840/SC1x－Supply－Chain－Fundamentals－－MITx－MicroMaster－s－Credential－in－Supply－Chain－Management/）

CHAPTER 17
Global Marketing and R&D

At the end of this chapter, you should be able to:

- Understand the marketing mix of international marketing;
- Discuss how thePEST model influence international marketing;
- How to vary the product attributes and vary advertising/ promoting strategies from country to country;
- Understand the great importance of international channel;
- Grasp on-filed tactics and approaches of channel management.

Case: Suppliers & Channel: Win-win or Zero-sum?

In China's retail industry, slotting fees (通道费) have become standard practice. But since their inception, they have been controversial. Supplier complained that the first time a product enters a supermarket, the suppliers need to pay "account fees"; for products displayed in prominent locations, we need to pay "standee fees"; for holiday promotions we need to pay "festival fees"...

In the 1990's, Carrefour, a French retail giant entered China, bringing its expansion model in developing countries: charging slotting fees, thereby tying up suppliers' money to earn back profits. The model helped Carrefour expand rapidly at low cost. At present, a vast majority of retail companies in China are using this low-cost, low-risk approach. In general, the giant retailer always take advantage of suppliers and impose a strict control on up-steam suppliers. Relying on their supply chain advantages, they charge various fees to suppliers to maintain a healthy cash flow. Suppliers' capital is occupied by supermarkets, and they have to pay high slotting fees, making their business more difficult. Name brand suppliers may have a chance of standing up for their rights and resisting the demands of retailers, but most domestic suppliers are small- or medium-sized enterprises, and they have no choice but to deal with it.

Retailers don't like this situation either. Pei Liang, secretary-general of China Chain Store & Franchise Association, believes that the retailer-supplier conflict is led by rising costs of commodities. As the price of products goes up rapidly, both sides get dissatisfied with the original conditions of contracts. In recent years, labor costs, utilities and rents have all gone up. Supermarkets and other retailers need the slotting fees to make up for their loss of profits, but manufacturers are also faced with the same problem, so conflicts may arise. If these don't get resolved, the situation will get worse.

What is the solution for retailer-supplier conflicts?

Reference: Lisa Hui. Slotting Fees: Product of Market Economy. http://cib.shangbao.net.cn/c/59664.html.

Discussion:

1. Please discuss the root and effects of retailer-supplier conflicts.

2. In general, the giant retailer always take advantage of suppliers and impose a strict control on up-steam suppliers. But can you propose some measures which the suppliers can use to counter-control of the retailers downstream?

Case: The Rebel of Nokia Channel Members (2011)

Nokia was once the world leading mobile phone supplier. Taking the edge of its state-of-art high technology, Nokia occupied 15.7% world market share of smart phone. But the story ended in April 2011, when Apple smart phone took 19.1% world market share and outrun Nokia for the first time.

There are many reasons for Apple's overtaking. But in China, Nokia made a great channel mistakes for a long time, which accelerate the collapse of Nokia. During the past decades, Nokia is a big name company and Nokia smart phone is best-seller in China. That is why when we examine the relationship between upstream supplier and downstream dealers of smart phone market, it is no doubt that the ups-stream supplier, Nokia, was in a dominant position and took advantage of the downstream dealers. For example, Nokia occupied the capital of dealers minimum for 6 months; if Nokia caught a dealer carrying out grey market (sourcing smart phones from the assigned area of other dealers and sell in his own territory), Nokia will fine (罚款) the dealer 10 000 RMB per phone without giving legal invoice. The Chinese dealers are under strict control of Nokia and are over-exploited by Nokia.

That is why since Since April, 2011, all the channel members of Nokia brand mobile phone in China say No to Nokia, refuse to take more smart phones from Nokia, and slash the price of Nokia phone inventory, as well as became enthusiastic about the distribution of Apple smart phone. The channel structure of Nokia smart phone collapsed immediately.

Reference：诺基亚中国市场渠道崩盘：大批代理商拒绝进货 http://tech.sina.com.cn/t/3g/2011-08-15/08105928010. shtml

Discussion：

1. The international channel are especially valuable and monopolistic. Please discuss with your partner how to approach channel objectives, how to design the length, width and depth of international channel?

2. Please use Nokia as an example, discuss with your partner the approaches/measures which the retailers/dealers control the suppliers? Ask you partner to propose some measures which the upstream supplier can use to counter-control of the retailers?

3. China (and Chinese companies) spent 861 Billion RMB (appx. US $ 130 Billion) in R&D in 2011, the second largest R&D investment in the world (The USA was No. 1). But there is a rumor and saying that Chinese firms just literally copy technology from foreign firms, So they get to manufacture the same product without the R&D costs. Could you make some comments on this saying?

Case：Fantastic Price Escalation (2014)

Bentley Motors Co. Limited（宾利汽车公司）, a British luxury car brand owned by Germany's Volkswagen, announced in July 2014 that it delivered 1 318 cars in the Chinese market in the first half of 2014, up 61 percent from the same period of 2013. The United States remains Bentley's number one market with 1 388 cars delivered to customers. But Wolfgang Durheimer, Chairman and CEO of Bentley, believes that China will overtake United States as the largest market for the company within 2014. Durheimer also said that Bentley plans to create eight flagship showrooms in major cities around the world, including two in China, and bring the world's first luxury SUV to the market in 2016, with first launch in Britain, then in the European continent, the United States and China consequently.

Most shocking is the price of such imported luxury car. Take Bentley GT4. 0 as an example, the price in USA and Europe is 160 000 USD, about 1 million RMB, but the price for the Chinese customers is 4 million RMB minimum.

Why there is a shocking price escalation of imported luxury car? First, of course is the high tariff barrier. The luxury car should pay tariff and VAT (value-added tax) 25% and 17%, respectively, consumption tax vary to 25%~40%. The total tax will amount to 146%. But even after paying 146% tax, the price of Bentley GT 4. 0 should be 1 (1+146%) = 2. 46 million RMB. But the sellingprice in China is 4 million minimum, there is still 1. 5 million RMB price gap. Taking the reasonable transportation cost etc. apart, there remaining the huge profit of dealers and the brand car suppliers. The soaring demand from domestic China push high the luxury car price. Bentley and Benz benefit greatly from China market, because about half (50%) of their global sale revue is from China. Compared to other fast-moving consumable goods giants, for example GE (General Electronics), China market only contribute 3% of its global sale revenue. Simple calculation may explain the recent two affairs：

1. In 2013, world luxury car brand, for example, Bentley, Benz, Renault already fired their Chinese dealers/agents (revocation of power of attorney) and take back the control of dealing rights and operation in China. In 2011, Volvo fired its Chinese dealer. In 2010, Land Rover fired its local dealers.

2. Since July 2014, National Development and Reform Commission further the anti-trust (反垄断) investigation on imported luxury cars, this investigation started in 2012, but for 3 years, nothing improvement achieved.

Reference：Bentley to see China as biggest market：chairman. http://www.chinadaily.com.cn/business/motoring/2014-07/25/content_17924170.htm

Discussion：

1. Please discuss the root, demonstration of international price escalation.

2. Could you propose some measures which can reduce /lower the international price escalation?

3. Why do some suppliers, such as Haier and Gree, prefer to set up their own channels/distribution facilities instead of cooperating with giant dealers for example Gome and Sunning?

Extended Reading：

1. Online documentary：Up-and -downstream of fast-moving consumable goods giants：P&G and Walmart. http://v.youku.com/v_show/id_XMTg1MDIyODA0.html；

2. Online news：The supplier collectively resist the ChinaRedstar 红星美凯龙（2009）；

Case：Carrefour Exited Worldwide?

France-based Carrefour SA, the world's second largest retailer by revenue, denied on Tuesday that it is considering selling its China business. But Similar rumors around Carrefour circulated in recent years.

But maybe it is not rumor. In 2014, Carrefour exited from India. In the 2012 Top 100 retail chain rankings (by the China chain store association), foreign competitors such as Walmart, and domestic retailers Brilliance Group and CR Vangard, outstripped Carrefour China. In 2012, Carrefour said it was pulling out of Singapore and Greece. Those markets are not the first that the French supermarket chain has left. In 2010, Carrefour sold its business in Thailand. In 2009, the company withdrew from the Russian marke. In 2005, Carrefour announced the sale of its operations in Japan and Mexico. In 2006, it sold its stores in South Korea. Aan industry analyst at Beijing United Innovation Capital Ltd, said："The company will not leave China in the short term, as growth of China's retail sector will be faster than in other world markets."

Reference：Carrefour source denies chain plans to exit market. http://www.chinadaily.com.cn/language_tips/cdaudio/2013-06/26/content_16661300.htm；

Discussion:

1. Why is Carrefour rumored to be leaving the Chinese market?

2. Why did Carrefour historically exit from many markets, such as Germany, Japan, Korea etc.?

International Success Tips:

The International Takeoff of New Products:

—the Role of Economics, Culture and Country Innovativeness

Global Marketing is a critical element for achieving international business success. Sales takeoff is vitally important for the management of new products. International marketer addresses the following questions about takeoff in Europe: (1) Does takeoff occur as distinctly in other countries? (2) Do different categories and countries have consistently different times-to-takeoff? (3) What economic and cultural factors explain the inter-country differences? (4) Should managers use a sprinkler or waterfall strategy for the introduction of new products across countries?

Gerard J. Tellis gathered data on 137 new products across 10 categories and 16 European countries. The major findings are as follows: (1) Sales of most new products display a distinct takeoff in various European countries, at an average of 6 years after introduction. (2) The time-to-takeoff varies substantially across countries and categories. It is four times shorter for entertainment products than for kitchen & laundry appliances. It is almost half as long in Scandinavian countries as in Mediterranean countries. (3) While culture partially explains inter-country differences in time-to-takeoff, economic factors are neither strong nor robust explanatory factors. (4) These results suggest distinct advantages to a waterfall strategy for introducing products in international markets.

Reference: Gerard J. Tellis. Marshall School of Business. http://international-business-center.com/international_marketing.html

Online Lectures by Top University:

1. Introduction to Marketing (University of Pennsylvania, http://mooc.guokr.com/course/580/Introduction-to-Marketing/)

2. Channel Management and Retailing (IE Business School, http://mooc.guokr.com/course/7883/Channel-Management-and-Retailing/)

CHAPTER 18
Global Human Resource Management

At the end of this chapter, you should be able to:

· Know the challenges of international human resource management;

· Understand the pros and cons of different approaches to staffing policy worldwide;

· Know why expatriate cost huge money and easily suffer failure;

· Understand the performance appraisal system and compensation system varies worldwide.

Case: Expatriate Failure: Time to Abandon?

Cohen (1977) define expatriate (外派) as voluntary, temporary migrant, mostly from affluent countries who resides abroad for one of the following reasons - business, teaching, research, culture and leisure.

Expatriate in international business is mostly expensive. To move a guy abroad, a company need provide anattractive expatriate package, career - related include giving greater responsibility and power; high base salary and incentives. Family-related include luxury accommodation, facilities for wife and his kids, even local several sports and social club membership to have a string of local society and friends. Why TNCs take pains and costs to send expatriate worldwide, because TNCs believe the expatriates can protect shareholders interests; help to maintain and spread the corporate culture; help HQ (headquarters) to control - will clearly follow HQ instructions because promotion depends on it; there is a shortage of home-country managers; there are a symbol of the company's commitment.

But international expatriate is mostly risky and suffer high failure rate more than 50%. Developers of training programs for international expatriate assignments must ask certain key questions amidst increasing globalization, most importantly: Why international assignments end in failure? This question addresses organizational anticipatory factors related to the effectiveness of selection mechanisms and criteria, in-country adjustment, and evaluation of expatriates. Attention should be paid to the challenges of complex international expatriate assignments by identifying the underlying variables that either positively or negatively influence the success and failure of foreign based organizations and expatriate performance. Furthermore, emphases should be put in the need for managing the performance of expatriates through careful selections, training, and compensation.

Discussion:

1. Why do international expatriates suffer high failure rate?

2. Could you and your partner propose some constructive measures which help a successfully expatriate?

3. The following chart is the selection mechanisms and criteria for UK and Germany TNCs to select their expatriate. Please make some comments on their criteria.

Marx (1996): Survey of UK and Germany Companies

Items	UK (%)	Germany (%)
International Competencies	20.1	15.6
Psychological Testing	15.2	4.4
Spouse Interview	4.3	15.3
Offer of Cultural Training	44.4	44.6
Mentor System	21.3	28.9
Guaranteed Re-entry job	35.6	88.8

Extended Reading Book:

Managing Cross Cultural Transition: A Handbook for Corporations, Employees, and Their Families

Case: Dell Executives Flee to Lenovo (2013)

In August 2013, it is a total shock and embarrassment for Dell, because in just two weeks, FIVE senior executives flee to its rivalry: Lenovo. Started by the President and CEO of Dell China fleeing to competitor, the following two weeks saw other four senior follow him. The senior executives of Dell China are now all in Lenovo.

There are only 17 Senior Vice President (Senior VP) in Lenovo, 9 of these senior executives are from the background of Dell or IBM. The working language in HQ is English. David D.

Miller（麦大伟），the ex- President and CEO of Dell China，took the role of Lenovo Asia and Pacific business；David Schmoock，the ex-vice-President of Dell Japan was appointed as the head of new-established "Excellent Center"，responsible for forecasting，pricing，selling and inventory management. Gerry P. Smith，the ex-VP of Dell，was responsible of Lenovo's global supply chain management（SCM）. While Mr. Liu Jun，the ex-executive for lobal SCM，was sent to university pursuing advanced training and skills.

Early in 2005，the Asia-Pacific President of Dell joined Lenovo and was appointed as President and CEO of Lenovo Group. Before him，a Dell's sales director joined Lenovo. In fact，Dell has become the executive nursing center for Lenovo.

Reference：王如晨. 戴尔高管连续空降联想. http://www.sina.com.cn 2006 年 09 月 12 日.

Discussion：

1. How do you look at the flee of Dell's senior executives?

2. The chairman of Dell said he will not besleepless with the flee. Because Dell has signed confidentiality agreement with all the executives，so Dell will not lose any commercial patents or secret. Please give some comments on his view.

Extended Reading：

Evaluation System of Performance and Compensation Package

CHAPTER 19
Accounting in the International Business

At the end of this chapter, you should be able to:

- Understand the differences in accounting standard s worldwide and their effects;
- Understand the emerging of international accounting standard and its implication;
- Understand how TNCs use accounting system to control business worldwide;
- Discuss why world top accounting & auditing firms were caught in fraud.

Case: Lever Temptation + Regulatory Indulgence: —Wall Street Fall on His Hands (2008)

Lehman Brothers Holdings Inc. (former NYSE ticker symbol LEH) was a global financial services firm. Before declaring bankruptcy in 2008, Lehman was the fourth-largest investment bank in the US (behind Goldman Sachs, Morgan Stanley, and Merrill Lynch), doing business in investment banking, equity and fixed-income sales and trading (especially U. S. Treasury securities), research, investment management, private equity, and private banking.

At 1: 45 AM on September 15, 2008, the firm filed for Chapter 11 Bankruptcy Protection following the massive exodus of most of its clients, drastic losses in its stock, and devaluation of its assets by credit rating agencies. Lehman's bankruptcy filing is the largest in US history, and is thought to have played a major role in the unfolding of the late-2000s global financial crisis. The following day, Barclays announced its agreement to purchase, subject to regulatory approval, Lehman's North American investment-banking and trading divisions along with its New York headquarters building. On September 20, 2008, a revised version of that agreement was approved by US Bankruptcy Court Judge James M. Peck. The next week, Nomura Holdings announced that it would acquire Lehman Brothers' franchise in the Asia-Pacific region, including Japan, Hong Kong and Australia, as well as Lehman Brothers' investment banking and equities businesses in Europe and the Middle East. The deal became effective on October 13, 2008.

A March 2010 report by the court-appointed examiner indicated that Lehman executives regularly used cosmetic accounting gimmicks at the end of each quarter to make its finances appear less shaky than they really were. This practice was a type of repurchase agreement that temporarily removed securities from the company's balance sheet. However, unlike typical repurchase agreements, these deals were described by Lehman as the outright sale of securities and created "a materially misleading picture of the firm's financial condition in late 2007 and 2008".

Early in August 2007 the firm closed its subprime lender, BNC Mortgage, eliminating 1 200 positions in 23 locations, and took an after-tax charge of $ 25 million and a $ 27 million reduction in goodwill. Lehman said that poor market conditions in the mortgage space "necessitated a substantial reduction in its resources and capacity in the subprime space". In 2008, Lehman faced an unprecedented loss to the continuing subprime mortgage crisis. Lehman's loss was a result of having held on to large positions in subprime and other lower-rated mortgage tranches when securitizing the underlying mortgages; whether Lehman did this because it was simply unable to sell the lower-rated bonds, or made a conscious decision to hold them, is unclear. In any event, huge losses accrued in lower-rated mortgage-backed securities throughout 2008. In the second fiscal quarter, Lehman reported losses of $ 2.8 billion and was forced to sell off $ 6 billion in assets. In the first half of 2008 alone, Lehman stock lost 73% of its value as the credit market continued to tighten. In August 2008, Lehman reported that it intended to release 6% of its work force, 1 500 people, just ahead of its third-quarter-reporting deadline in September.

In September 2007, Joe Gregory appointed Erin Callan as CFO. On March 16, 2008, after rival Bear Stearns was taken over by JP Morgan Chase in a fire sale, market analysts suggested that Lehman would be the next major investment bank to fall.

Callan fielded Lehman's first quarter conference call, where the firm posted a profit of $ 489 million, compared to Citigroup's $ 5.1 billion and Merrill Lynch's $ 1.97 billion losses which was Lehman's 55th consecutive profitable quarter. The firm's stock price leapt 46 percent after that announcement. On June 9, 2008, Lehman Brothers announced US $ 2.8 billion second-quarter loss, its first since being spun off from American Express, as market volatility rendered many of its hedges ineffective during that time. Lehman also reported that it had raised a further $ 6 billion in capital. As a result, there was major management shakeup, when Hugh "Skip" McGee III (head of investment banking) held a meeting with senior staff to strip Fuld and his lieutenants of their authority. Consequently, Joe Gregory agreed to resign as President and COO, and afterward he told Erin Callan that she had to resign as CFO. Callan was appointed CFO of Lehman in 2008 but served only for six months, before departing after her mentor Joe Gregory was demoted. Bart McDade was named to succeed Gregory as President and COO, when several senior executives threatened to leave if he was not promoted. McDade took charge and brought back Michael Gelband and Alex Kirk, who had previously been pushed out of the firm by Gregory for not taking risks. Although Fuld remained CEO, he soon became isolated from McDade's team. On August 22, 2008, shares in Lehman closed up 5% (16% for the week) on reports that the state-controlled Korea Development Bank was considering buying the bank. Most of those gains were quickly eroded as news came in that Korea Development Bank was "facing difficulties pleasing regulators and attracting partners for the deal". It culminated on September 9, when Lehman's shares plunged 45% to \$ 7.79, after it was reported that the state-run South Korean firm had put talks on hold.

On September 17, 2008 Swiss reestimated its overall net exposure to Lehman Brothers as approximately CHF 50 million. Investor confidence continued to erode as Lehman's stock lost roughly half its value and pushed the S&P 500 down 3.4% on September 9. The Dow Jones lost 300 points the same day on investors' concerns about the security of the bank. The U. S. government did not announce any plans to assist with any possible financial crisis that emerged at Lehman. The next day, Lehman announced a loss of \$ 3.9 billion and its intent to sell off a majority stake in its investment-management business, which includes Neuberger Berman. The stock slid seven percent that day. Lehman, after earlier rejecting questions on the sale of the company, was reportedly searching for a buyer as its stock price dropped another 40 percent on September 11, 2008.

Just before the collapse of Lehman Brothers, executives at Neuberger Berman sent e-mail memos suggesting, among other things, that the Lehman Brothers' top people forgo multi-million dollar bonuses to "send a strong message to both employees and investors that management is not shirking accountability for recent performance". Lehman Brothers Investment Management Director George Herbert Walker IV dismissed the proposal, going so far as to actually apologize to other members of the Lehman Brothers executive committee for the idea of bonus reduction having been suggested. He wrote, "Sorry team. I am not sure what's in the water at Neuberger Berman. I'm embarrassed and I apologize."

During hearings on the bankruptcy filing by Lehman Brothers and bailout of AIG before the House Committee on Oversight and Government Reform, former Lehman Brothers CEO Richard Fuld said a host of factors including a crisis of confidence and naked short-selling attacks followed by false rumors contributed to both the collapse of Bear Stearns and Lehman Brothers.

Reference: http://en.wikipedia.org/wiki/Lehman_Brothers

Discussion:

1. Could you specify the accounting gimmicks used by Lehman Brothers to window dressing its financial statement? How these tricks work to doctor the accounting books and conceal he huge accounting risks?

2. Since 1990s, at the push of Wall Street, USA began so - called "financial deregulation" reform. Which means almost free hand on innovated financial products and business. How do you think this regulatory indulgence lead to the bankruptcy of Lehman Brothers and the 2008 global financial crisis ?

Case: Enron Scandal (2001): Audit Failure

The Enron scandal, revealed in October 2001, eventually led to the bankruptcy of the Enron Corporation, an American energy company based in Houston, Texas. The scandal lead to the dissolve of Arthur Andersen, which was one of the five largest audit and accountancy partnerships in the world. In addition to being the largest bankruptcy reorganization in American history at that time, Enron was attributed as the biggest audit failure.

Enron was formed in 1985 by Kenneth Lay after merging Houston Natural Gas and InterNorth. Several years later, when Jeffrey Skilling was hired, he developed a staff of executives that, by the use of accounting loopholes, special purpose entities, and poor financial reporting, were able to hide billions of dollars in debt from failed deals and projects. Chief Financial Officer Andrew Fastow and other executives not only misled Enron's board of directors and audit committee on high-risk accounting practices, but also pressured Andersen to ignore the issues . Enron hired numerous Certified Public Accountants (CPAs) as well as accountants who had worked on developing accounting rules with the Financial Accounting Standards Board (FASB). The accountants searched for new ways to save the company money, including capitalizing on loopholes found in Generally Accepted Accounting Principles (GAAP), the accounting industry's standards. One Enron accountant revealed, "We tried to aggressively use the literature (GAAP) to our advantage. All the rules create all these opportunities. We got to where we did because we exploited that weakness."

Enron shareholders filed a $40 billion lawsuit after the company's stock price, which achieved a high of US $90.75 per share in mid-2000, plummeted to less than $1 by the end of November 2001. The U. S. Securities and Exchange Commission (SEC) began an investigation, and rival Houston competitor Dynegy offered to purchase the company at a very low price. The deal failed, and on December 2, 2001, Enron filed for bankruptcy under Chapter 11 of the United States Bankruptcy Code. Enron's $63.4 billion in assets made it the largest corporate bankruptcy in U. S. history until WorldCom's bankruptcy in 2002.

Many executives at Enron were indicted for a variety of charges and were later sentenced to prison. Enron's auditor, Arthur Andersen, was found guilty in a United States District Court, but by the time the ruling was overturned at the U. S. Supreme Court, the company had lost the majority of its customers and had ceased operating. Employees and shareholders received limited returns in lawsuits, despite losing billions in pensions and stock prices. As a consequence of the scandal, new regulations and legislation were enacted to expand the accuracy of financial reporting for public companies. One piece of legislation, the Sarbanes-Oxley Act, increased penalties for destroying, altering, or fabricating records in federal investigations or for attempting to defraud shareholders. The act also increased the accountability of auditing firms to remain unbiased and independent of their clients.

Reference: http://en.wikipedia.org/wiki/Enron_scandal

Discussion:

1. Could you specify the gimmicks used by Enron to window dress its accounting books, for example, the use of accounting loopholes, special purpose entities (SPV), and poor financial reporting etc. How the tricks work?

2. Enron hired numerous Certified Public Accountants (CPAs) as well as accountants who had worked on developing accounting rules with the Financial Accounting Standards Board (FASB). One Enron accountant revealed "We tried to aggressively use the literature (GAAP) to our advantage". How do you look at this strange but not unique accounting and auditing phenomena worldwide?

3. Please discuss why Arthur Andersen, the outsider auditor and big name giant accounting form, failed to audit Enron properly? The auditor took huge auditing fees from Enron and in fact Enron is a VIP customer and in fact a benefactor of Arthur Anderson. How can such form act as an independent outsider auditor? What is the ethical and political dilemma in such situation?

Online Practices:

1. Please search on internet the successive accounting and auditing laws and regulations which were implemented after the Enron Scandal. For example.

2. Sarbanes- Oxley Act (2002), also known as the "Public Company Accounting Reform and Investor Protection Act" (in the Senate) and "Corporate and Auditing Accountability and Responsibility Act" (in the House), OR in short SOX.

Case: BP: From Oil Spilling to Financial Reform Killing (2010)

Oil giant BP may be overwhelmed with the clean-up from the collapse of its Deepwater oil rig in the Gulf of Mexico. But the corporation has still found time to fight tougher financial reforms on Capitol Hill. The corporation is a member of the Coalition for Derivatives End-Users, a collection of companies actively pushing for a loophole in new regulations governing derivatives, the complex and opaque products used to hedge risk and bet on fluctuations in the financial markets. Derivatives, experts say, exacerbated the 2008 financial crisis, and lawmakers and the White House have sought to drag that market into the sunlight. The financial reform legislation now in Congress, says President Obama, will "close the loopholes that allowed derivatives deals so large and risky they could threaten our entire economy".

Not if BP has its way. The corporation, along with the US Chamber of Commerce, Business Roundtable, and other large advocacy groups, wants to ensure that it is exempted from a new provision in derivatives regulation that would increase transparency and make derivatives trading less risky. (BP did not respond to a request for comment.)

First, a primer on the derivatives regulation on the table. The House and Senate bills would mandate that derivatives be traded on an exchange, just as stocks are. This would mean that information on the structure, volume, and pricing of derivatives deals are out in the open. If you're an airline trying to hedge against the fluctuations in the cost of jet fuel, you'd be able to look at what your competitors paid and get the same kind of deal—not pay an amount devised by a Wall Street broker looking to make a killing. "Transparency brings better pricing and lowers risk for all parties to a derivatives transaction," says Gary Gensler, chairman of the

Commodity Futures Trading Commission.

But what's got BP upset is a proposal to force derivatives togo through a clearinghouse, a central body that would act as a middleman on each trade, collect data, and help protect failed derivatives deals from leading to massive losses that harm the wider economy. The clearinghouse would do so by requiring companies in a trade to put forward money or other collateral in case those trades went wrong. This, lawmakers and finance experts say, is crucial: Without this middleman ensuring everyone can deliver on their bets, the likely result is another AIG-like meltdown, when a company enters into so many trades that it can't afford to cover them all if they all fail.

BP doesn't want to front up cash or collateral when it trades in derivatives. "These additional costs will impact the ability of these companies to meet their financial obligations, threaten needed job creation, and significantly weaken the ability of American companies to compete globally." the Coalition for Derivatives End-Users wrote in a April 28, 2010, letter urging Congress to include an exemption for end-users, the non-financial companies that use derivatives as part of their business practices of hedging risk (the letter was signed by the American Petroleum Institute, of which BP Americais a member). In addition to its membership in the end-users coalition, BP America hired the Podesta Group, a powerful Washington firm, to lobby this year on derivatives and other financial reform issues on Capitol Hill, according to the Center for Responsive Politics.

According to the Congressional Research Service (CRS), an end-user exemption could undercut derivatives legislation as a whole. A December 2009 CRS report stated, "Nearly two-thirds of OTC derivatives involve an end user. If all end users are exempted from the requirement that OTC swaps be cleared, the market structure problems raised by AIG still remain." Financial reform advocates charged BP with lobbying to defeat vital reform. "We think the idea of an end-user exemption is just unacceptable in terms of creating more transparency in the system," says Lauren Weiner with Americans for Financial Reform. "Anyone who's pushing for those opt-out provisions should take a close look at the really positive benefits of putting these trades in the sunlight."

BP's efforts, however, have partly paid off. In the House's financial reform legislation, BP, via the end-user coalition, sent letters to every member of Congress lobbying for an exemption—which it ultimately won. BP claimed that because it isn't heavily involved in derivatives trading, it shouldn't be affected by the bill, says a spokeswoman for the Senate Agriculture Committee, Courtney Rowe.

On the Senate side, Rowe added, BP wouldn't get its way. Sen. Blanche Lincoln (D-ark.), the architect of the Senate's tough derivatives proposals, has rejected BP's claims and others like it, and has fought against loopholes in new derivatives rules. "Senator Lincoln felt that regardless of the amount of swap dealing you do," Rowe wrote in an email to *Mother Jones*, "If you're a swap dealer you should be regulated as one."

Reference: Andy Kroll. BP: From Oil Spilling to Financial Reform Killing. http://www.motherjones.com/politics/2010/05/bp-oil-spilling-financial-reform-killing

Discussion:

How the giant TNC s as Bp etc. and financial elites from Wall street influence the financial de-regulation reform in USA? It is said that financial de-regulation lead directly to the boom of various complicated and high risky derivatives, thus the world financial crisis such as 2008. Please discuss with your partners about this issue.

Case: Ernst & Young Caught in Tax Evasion (2013)

Tax evasion is the illegal evasion oftaxes by individuals, corporations and trusts. Tax evasion often entails taxpayers deliberately misrepresenting the true state of their affairs to the tax authorities to reduce their tax liability and includes dishonest tax reporting, such as declaring less income, profits or gains than the amounts actually earned, or overstating deductions. Tax evasion is an activity commonly associated with the informal economy. One measure of the extent of tax evasion (the "tax gap") is the amount of unreported income, which is the difference between the amount of income that should be reported to the tax authorities and the actual amount reported.

In contrast, tax avoidance is the legal use of tax laws to reduce one's tax burden. Both tax evasion and avoidance can be viewed as forms of tax noncompliance, as they describe a range of activities that intend to subvert a state's tax system, although such classification of tax avoidance is not indisputable, given that avoidance is lawful, within self-creating systems. Although the definitions of tax evasion and avoidance is clear, but in practices, there is blurring between the two.

In March 2013, the Big Four accounting firm, Ernst & Young (安永) agreed to pay federal prosecutors $ 123 million to settle criminal tax avoidance charges stemming from $ 2 billion in unpaid taxes from about 200 wealthy individuals advised by four Ernst & Young senior partners between 1999 and 2004.

The deal, which ensures the internationalaccountancy firm will not face criminal prosecution, marks the end of a tax avoidance scandal that hung over E&Y for several years. The episode saw four former employees sentenced in 2010 to between 20 and 36 months in jail for involvement in tax evasion and obstructing the US Internal Revenue Service (IRS). Two last year had their convictions overturned on appeal. The four had been core members of a small E&Y unit called Viper - Value Ideas Produce Extraordinary Results - set up in 1999 to devise tax strategies to market to wealthy individuals looking to shelter incomes of more than $ 20m from the taxman. E&Y admitted that products developed from the Viper division - one of which was called Currency Options Bring Reward Alternatives, or Cobra - had been designed to appear to the IRS as genuine investments when, in reality, the products were designed and marketed to clients as a series of pre-planned steps that would defer, reduce or eliminate tax bills for millionaire clients. In order to trick the IRS, E&Y admitted its former tax experts went to great lengths not to create documents that would make clear the tax motives behind their complex strategies. The $ 123m. penalty agreed with Manhattan US attorney Preet Bharara is the same amount as E&Y received in fees on the four admitted avoidance structures it developed and marketed in conjunction with law firms, banks and investment advisers. E&Y said it was: "pleased to put this matter from a decade ago behind us" and gave undertakings not to get involved in such schemes again.

Reference: Ernst & Young to pay US regulators $ 123m. over tax avoidance schemes. http://www.theguardian.com/business/2013/mar/03/ernst-young-pays-us-regulators

Case: Entrepreneur Accused of Biggest-Ever Tax Scam (2013) —Telecom Investor Charged with Failing to Pay $ 200 Million

On June 28, 2013, The Justice Department filed its biggest personal tax evasion case ever, accusing the man who once tried to rescue Russia's Mir space station, Walter Anderson, of failing to pay more than $ 200 million in personal income taxes by stashing income in offshore bank accounts. The allegations mark the largest criminal tax case against an individual, said Mark Everson, commissioner of the Internal Revenue Service. Anderson, 51, earned millions by dealing in telecommunications companies after the AT&T breakup and became a global figure about five years ago when he embarked on a mission to rescue the ailing Mir space station. The Justice Department arrested him over the weekend at Dulles International Airport as he was returning on a flight from London. A grand jury indictment accuses him of, over a five-year period, conducting business through offshore corporations in Panama and the British Virgin Islands to make it appear he was not personally earning the income. Those ventures earned nearly a half billion dollars. Anderson pleaded not guilty to the tax evasion charges Monday and was ordered held without bail until a hearing. If convicted on all the charges, he could face up to 80 years in prison. This case is part of a recent push by federal prosecutors to crack down on use of offshore accounts to evade U. S. taxes. Five years ago, Anderson put up $ 20 million to try to salvage Mir, destined to burn up on eventual re-entry. He hoped to lease it to drug companies or firms interested in micro-gravity research, but the only market that showed any promise was space tourism. Dennis Tito, a high-rolling investor, agreed to pay over $ 20 million for a visit to Mir to become the world's first space tourist. And reality TV producer Mark Burnett signed a contract with MirCorp for a show, "Destination: Mir." Contestants would train in Russia, with the winner getting a trip to the space station. The Associated Press contributed to this report.

Another tax evasion was in Jan. 2012. US Charges 3 Swiss Bankers in Tax Evasion. Prosecutors accused three Swiss bankers of conspiring with wealthy U. S. taxpayers to hide more than $ 1. 2 billion in assets from tax authorities, and sources briefed on the matter said the three worked for Wegelin & Co, one of Switzerland's oldest private banks. The office of the

Manhattan U. S. Attorney said in a statement that the indictment charges the bankers with trying to "capture business lost by UBS and another large international Swiss bank in the wake of widespread news reports that the Internal Revenue Service was investigating UBS" in 2008 and 2009.

The charges signal that U. S. authorities are moving closer to criminal charges against some Swiss and Swiss-style banks that sold tax evasion services to rich Americans, according to the sources.

Wegelin was not identified in the single indictment filed against Michael Berlinka, Urs Frei and Roger Keller. The three men, who reside in Switzerland, worked for the unnamed between 2005 and 2010 and sold tax evasion services from the bank's Zurich office. Wegelin, a small bank owned by its managing partners, does not have a United States presence, and the bank carried out its work for approximately 100 U. S. clients through a Stamford, Connecticut, branch of UBS, the giant Swiss bank, according to the indictment. Wegelin "directly accessed the U. S. banking system through a correspondent bank account held at UBS," which the indictment said was in Stamford, Connecticut. Wegelin could not immediately be reached for comment. If convicted, the bankers face a maximum prison term of five years under the conspiracy charge.

Reference: Entrepreneur accused of biggest-ever tax scam Telecom investor charged with failing to pay $ 200 million, http://www.nbcnews.com/id/7046153/

http://www.cnbc.com/id/45854768;

Extended Reading: China and US Agree to Curb Tax Evasion (2014)

On June 26, 2014, China and USA agreed to cub tax evasion. The agreement between China and the United States for US financial accounts registered at banks in China to send their tax reports to the US Internal Revenue Services (IRS) to curb offshore tax evasion. The agreement will also enable Beijing to obtain information on mainland taxpayers in the US to help fight against tax evasion and corruption.

The wealthy in China are obtaining foreign nationalities for their children and spouses to illicitly transfer income to foreign financial institutions in an attempt to escape tax reviews by the Chinese government. Under the agreement, US financial accounts will report their taxes directly to the Chinese government, which will then file them to the IRS. In the past, the accounts were only required to be reported to the foreign country's government.

The two countries agreed on the terms, but are reviewing before officially signing it. The new agreement will remove the threat of blacklisting or penalties that have been hanging over Chinese financial institutions, including institutions in Hong Kong, the US and other subsidiaries in the Chinese mainland.

The US government's implementation of the 2010 Foreign Account Tax Compliance Act (FATCA) is to curb offshore taxes that were previously not reported. Around 80 000 banks and other financial institutions have agreed to start reporting to the IRS on US-owned foreign accounts by July 1.

FATCA is a US law that requires financial institutions around the world to provide information on US taxpayers to the US government. The Treasury Department said on its website that Beijing had reached an "in substance" intergovernmental agreement Model 1 (IGA 1) with the US.

Under the Act, financial firms around the world are required to report to the IRS information on clients who are US taxpayers. Those that fail to do so would face a 30-percent withholding tax on their US income. The law's definition of a "US person" includes green-card holders and anyone with a substantial connection to the country.

Agreements have been signed by the US with governments in 80 countries including almost all major economies. The agreements will allow banks to turn over account information to their governments instead of handing it directly to the US - a potential violation of privacy rules in some countries. In the past, Chinese officials expressed concerns about the potential burdens of complying with FATCA. The US has used intergovernmental agreements to simplify compliance. The conclusion of a model 1 IGA with China is a very significant development, the IGA will remove obstacles to compliance with FATCA and will allow Chinese financial institutions to avoid withholding under FATCA through direct reporting of information to the Chinese government. FATCA is aimed at shutting down tax planning by US persons that avoid US tax by shifting income to non-US banks outside of the visibility of the IRS. This tax planning is primarily directed towards lower tax jurisdictions such as Switzerland.

Reference: Elizabeth Wu. China & US agree to curb tax evasion. http://www.chinadaily.com.cn/world/2014-06/30/content_17623410.htm

Discussion:

1. How do you look at the blurring of tax avoidance and tax evasion?

2. Why were the top accounting firms, such as Ernst & Young (安永), involved in tax evasion scandal?

3. What tricks and techniques have you learned from the above two case? How do wealthy individuals and TNCs worldwide use these gimmicks ?

Chapter Discussion:

1. In tax appliance, there are many model, fro example TAG models, which said the Taxpayer As Gambler. But the puzzle of TAG and firms is that the firm seems to have disappeared. Because the taxpayer write out FOC, or solve for output and profits, or back into an "Allingham-Sandmo" world (分析逃税行为的经典理论).

2. The cat-and-mouse model is a reporting game model, in which the tax-payer and tax authority (TA) are with or without pre-commitment. Could you discuss these problems as: Is cat-and-mouse a suitable for firms? Is simple reporting models be appropriate ? Does the model omit some of the key strategic aspects of the game?

3. What is APA (advance pricing arrangement) with the tax authority? Please search internet to find more cases which is signed between TNCs from worldwide with the Chinese tax authorities.

4. The boss of LVMH flee to BELGIUM, because Hollande, the president of France, enacted 75% billionaire tax in Dec. 2013. How can the wealthy billionaires evade tax worldwide? Please devise the network-using and main approaches.

Online-extended reading book:

Ernst & Young Tax Guide 2013

Online Lectures by Top University:

1. Accounting for Business Decision Making: Measurement and Operational Decisions (University of Illinois at Urbana - Champaign, http://mooc.guokr.com/course/8133/Accounting-for-Business-Decision-Making--Measurement-and-Operational-Decisions/)

2. 会计与管理控制常见问题（HEC 等商学院，http://open.163.com/special/opencourse/management.html）

CHAPTER 20 Financial Management in the International Business

At the end of this chapter, you should be able to:

· Understand the role of financial choices in corporate strategy;

· Understand the principles underlying financial decision making in firms;

· Evaluate the principles in the light of evidence on firms' financial strategies and decisions;

· Apply principles to financial strategy in actual case studies;

· Compare firms' financial strategies across countries and historic periods;

· Critically discuss the problems and limitations of financial strategy techniques.

Case: What's Going Wrong at Sears Now? (2014)

The more merchandise a department store carries, the better. Broad inventory filled with brand names boosts a retailer's chances of "giving the lady what she wants" —the key to success, according to none other than Marshall Field. So it can't be a good sign that Converse Inc. has stopped selling shoes to Sears Holdings Corp. Nor is it a good sign that companies that insure supplier payments are tightening policies on sales to Sears, or that the cost of credit protection on the retailer's debt has risen to its highest level since 2012.

To be sure, Sears faces no holiday-season money crunch. But these actions suggest a deepening concern about the company's inability to make money from its stores and increasing reliance on asset sales to generate cash. "When one player starts to get worried (and pulls out), that's something that can potentially spread fast," says Steven Dennis, an independent retail consultant in Dallas and former Sears vice president. "People are very worried about getting stuck with a lot of liability."

Sears dismisses the disappearance of Converse from its shoe departments over the past few months as a non-event. The break was a mutual decision, a spokeswoman for the Hoffman Estates-based chain says. "While the brand name was appealing to carry, it did not represent a significant number of (products), nor was it material to our business," she writes in an email. She adds that consumers still can purchase Converse products at Sears Marketplace, a website it hosts for third-party sellers.

Converse is a wholly owned subsidiary of Nike Inc. The Beaverton, Oregon-based athletic-apparel giant made a similar decision to withdraw from Sears in 2005, when CEO Edward

Lampert merged the company with Kmart. At the time, the parting of ways was described as a brand management issue, as insiders speculated Nike did not want its shoes sold at discounter Kmart.

Converse Sneakers

Converse, which generated $ 1.45 billion in sales in fiscal 2013, is expected to nearly double sales to $ 3 billion by 2017, according to Nike. The company did not respond to requests for comment. For its part, Sears lost $ 1.37 billion in the year ended Feb. 1 as revenue slid 9 percent to $ 36.19 billion. Analysts expect it to lose money through fiscal 2015 and 2016. Its shares closed at $ 37.27 on Aug. 1, flat from a year earlier.

"SLOW PAY"

A big brand's decision to end its relationship with a retailer—regardless of its impact on the retailer's bottom line—could spring from a number of factors. The biggest cause of worry, of course, would be if the retailer had started to pay its vendors late, an action known as "slow pay". Sears did not respond to a question as to whether it paid Converse on time. A divorce also may arise from frustration if the retailer stops buying a sufficient breadth of a company's products and cherry-picks only its most popular items. Finally, a supplier may call it quits if it believes "the manner in which the goods are being sold is unacceptable," says Mark Cohen, director of retail studies at Columbia University's Graduate School of Business and a former president of Sears Canada who was forced out after a power struggle in 2004. "I suspect Converse is simply saying, 'This is not a place we think represents a legitimate platform for our brand.' "

Reasons Big Brands Walk Away From A Retailer

· Retailer pays its vendors late.

· Retailer stops buying a sufficient breadth of a company's products and cherry-picks only its most popular items.

· Retailer sells the goods in an unacceptable manner.

Analysts and retail experts agree that Converse was not a significant seller at Sears and that, despite its continued losses, the retailer is in no short-term danger of being unable to pay its bills.

Sears is relatively flush with cash thanks to a flurry of store closures, real estate sales and asset spinoffs. For the quarter ended May 3, it had reserves of $ 842 million, down from $ 1 billion from a year earlier. The company generated about $ 4 billion in cash altogether in 2012 and 2013, and says it will raise another $ 1 billion this year by selling its 51 percent stake in Sears Canada and its Sears Auto Centers. Moreover, Sears still can borrow $ 752 million under its $ 3.73 billion line of credit. Even so, the cost of credit protection on Sears' debt has been rising since February, when the company reported its loss for fiscal 2014, according to New York-based Strategies Research Partners. Meantime, insurance companies are tightening the policies they grant Sears suppliers: American International Group Inc. has cut the size of new policies by as much as half, according to Bloomberg News. With less insurance available, companies may cut sales or even stop working with Sears, analysts say. Gary Balter, an analyst at Credit Suisse in New York, wrote in May that Sears' announcement of the intention to sell its Sears Canada interest just before releasing a $ 402 million first-quarter loss could be interpreted as "sending a message to suppliers not to worry, as the cash flow deficit will once again be offset by a capital transaction." One day, however, Sears will run out of assets to sell. "Strategically, Sears is very challenged and hasn't shown any evidence of turning the corner," Mr. Dennis says. "There's a day of reckoning at some point."

Reference: Brigid Sweeney. Chicago Business. http://www.chicagobusiness.com/article/20140802/ISSUE01/308029971/whats-going-wrong-at-sears-now

Extended Reading: Corporate Finance and Career Requirements

Broadly speaking, corporate finance refers to all the financial activities of a private business. Often, the phrase is used more specifically to describe the fundraising and investing activities of a corporation. What's more, corporate finance refers to the more day-to-day accounting activities of a business, like accounts payable and accounts receivable, and higher-level strategic financial analysis.

Corporate finance and accounting professionals are responsible for managing a business's money—forecasting where it will come from, knowing where it is, and helping its managers decide how to spend it in ways that will ensure the greatest return. A company's size, complexity, industry, and stage of development (e. g., start-up or established business) determine its corporate finance department's specific responsibilities. All companies need to balance their books. But some large technology companies, for example, also need to hire financial experts to valuate potential acquisitions. Others (e. g., insurance companies) have hundreds of millions of dollars to invest and need financial wizards to manage that money.

Accounting concerns itself with day-to-day operations. Accountants balance the books, track expenses and revenue, execute payroll, and pay the bills. They also compile all the financial data needed to issue a company's financial statements in accordance with government regulations. Finance professionals analyze revenue and expenses to ensure effective use of capital. They also advise businesses about project costs, make capital investments, and structure deals to help companies grow. In spite of their different roles, finance and accounting are joined at the hip: The higher levels of accounting (budgeting and analysis) blend with financial functions (analysis and projections). Thus, finance and accounting are often treated as one, with different divisions undertaking particular tasks, such as cash management or taxes.

Requirements

Finance and accounting jobs require strong analytical and quantitative skills. If you have a knack for using numbers to understand patterns that influence business, you'll be of great value to your employer. If you can't crunch and analyze numbers, this isn't going to be the right job for you. You should also enjoy and excel at solving problems and be able to think critically about the numbers you're working with. To succeed in these careers, you also need a strong attention to detail. To make wise business decisions, your employer will be depending on you to get the numbers right – every time. To work in finance, you'll also need business acumen. This may be the career for you if you can effectively evaluate business scenarios and recommend a course of action based on quantitative research. If you're in college and you want to work in corporate finance, your best bet is to demonstrate your interest in finance with relevant undergraduate courses in accounting, finance, and economics. Internships are always a great way to strengthen your resume and differentiate yourself from other candidates. An MBA will make you attractive to companies hiring for budgeting, planning, and strategy functions. Many firms hire outstanding undergraduates and MBAs for training programs: Some are finance and accounting specific, and others rotate trainees throughout the company.

If you have your heart set on corporate finance and analysis, do a knockout job during that particular rotation and develop a good relationship with your manager. If there is no formal finance or accounting program at your company, you'll have to make the most of on-the-job training, so try to find a position that will expose you to a variety of projects. Find out what the career path in corporate finance is at your company and cultivate a mentor. A mentor can explain what projects will round out your background and what courses you can take to prepare yourself for a higher level assignment. You can also check out job listings on the web to see what kind of experience and certification the jobs you're interested in require. If you want to pursue a lifelong career as a number-cruncher, you'll probably have to knuckle down and get an advanced degree or certification—a CPA, MBA, or CFA, depending on the career—at least to work in the more senior budgeting, planning, and strategy functions. You'll also need to keep track of the regulatory changes that affect how information is reported. There are other ways to get your foot in the door in a corporate finance career. Experience with an investment banking firm can lead to a financial-analysis position for a specific business line or to a corporate-development position if you have several years of experience. At the higher levels in accounting, one of the most straightforward routes to becoming a controller (a supervisory accounting role) is to start working for one of the large accounting or auditing firms and then go into corporate finance. The largest accounting firms and investment banks hire BAs directly from school.

Career Tracks

Although conditions vary at different companies, people going into corporate finance generally start their careers either as staff accountants (for the corporate-reporting function) or as financial analysts (for a business group or function). In both roles, you'll supply management with the information it needs to make smart, opportune decisions.

Staff accountants consolidate information for the official corporate financial reports—primarily comparing the present to the past. Financial analysts, on the other hand, are assigned to either a product line or business unit. They help management in setting up profit objectives, analyzing current unit results, and anticipating future financial performance. Over time, financial analysts and staff accountants eventually specialize in one of the areas described below: General Accounting, Internal Audit, Divisional Financial Services, Tax, Treasury, Cash Management, Corporate Development and Strategic Planning.

Discussion:

1. The following is the compensation system calculated by Wetfoot www.wetfoot.com, please compare it within the context of Chinese companies.

Corporate finance compensation will vary by region, size of company, and industry. Following are typical salary ranges for a variety of corporate finance functions:

Chief financial officer:	$ 85 000 to $ 350 000
Treasurer:	$ 85 000 to $ 200 000
Controller/Finance director:	$ 60 000 to $ 190 000
Cash manager:	$ 50 000 to $ 90 000
Financial analyst:	$ 35 000 to $ 110 000
Accounts payable manager:	$ 40 000 to $ 75 000
Accountant:	$ 40 000 to $ 65 000
Credit analyst:	$ 25 000 to $ 70 000
Bookkeeping manager:	$ 25 000 to $ 80 000

2. Wizard, Inc. has a subsidiary in a country where the government allows only a mall amount of earnings to be remitted to the U. S. each year. Should Wizard finance the subsidiary with debt financing by the parent, equity financing by the parent, or financing by local banks in the foreign country?

3. Describe general differences between the capital structures of firms based in the United States and those of firms based in Japan. Offer an explanation for these differences. Discussion: Should the Reduced Tax Rate on Dividends Affect an MNC's Capital Structure?

4. Explain why an MNC parent would consider financing from its subsidiaries. Explain how a firm's degree of risk aversion enters into its decision of whether to finance in a foreign currency or a local currency.

5. Discussion: Will MNCs Increase Their Risk When Borrowing Foreign Currencies?

6. Discuss the general functions involved in international cash management. Explain how the MNC's optimization of cash flow can distort the profits of each subsidiary. Explain the benefits of NETTING. How can a centralized cash management system be beneficial to the MNC?

7. Discussion: Should Interest Rate Parity Prevent MNCs From Investing in Foreign Currencies?

Extended Reading Books:

1. Brealey R & Myers S. *Principles of corporate finance*. 10th edition. New York: McGraw Hill, 2011.

2. Hillier D, M Grinblatt, S Titman. *Financial markets and corporate strategy* (2nd edition). NewYork: McGraw Hill, 2011.

3. Koller T, M. Goedhart, D Wessels. *Valuation: measuring and managing the value of companies* (5th edition). New Jersey: Wiley, 2010.

Online Lectures by Top University:

1. Introduction to Corporate Finance (University of Pennsylvania, http://mooc.guokr.com/course/593/Introduction-to-Corporate-Finance/)

2. Financial Evaluation and Strategy: Corporate Finance (University of Illinois at Urbana, http://mooc.guokr.com/course/4391/Financial-Evaluation-and-Strategy--Corporate-Finance/)

3. Corporate Financial Policy (University of Michigan, http://mooc.guokr.com/course/8076/Corporate-Financial-Policy/)

